MEDIATING INTERNATIONAL CHILD ABDUCTION CASES

There is growing enthusiasm for the use of mediation to seek to resolve cases arising under the Hague Convention of 25 October 1980 on the Civil Aspects of International Child Abduction (the Convention). However, despite being endorsed by the conclusions of meetings of experts, judicial comment and even legislative changes, there have been relatively few cases where mediation has played a significant role. It is suggested that the reason underlying this dichotomy between the widespread support for the use of mediation and the current limited practice is that there are several key questions regarding the use of mediation in the context of the Convention which remain to be answered. Specifically: what is meant by Convention mediation? How can a mediation process fit within the constraints of the Convention? And why offer mediation in Convention cases given the existing legal framework? This book addresses these questions and in so doing seeks to encourage a movement from enthusiasm about the use of mediation in the Convention context to greater practice.

Volume 7 in the series Studies in Private International Law

Studies in Private International Law

Volume 1: Electronic Consumer Contracts in the Conflict of Laws
Sophia Tang

Volume 2: Foreign Currency Claims in the Conflict of Laws
Vaughan Black

Volume 3: Jurisdiction and Judgments in Relation to EU Competition Law Claims
Mihail Danov

Volume 4: International Commercial Disputes: Commercial Conflict of Laws in English Courts
Jonathan Hill and Adeline Chong

Volume 5: Cases and Materials on EU Private International Law
Stefania Bariatti

Volume 6: International Child Abduction: The Inadequacies of the Law
Thalia Kruger

Volume 7: Mediating International Child Abduction Cases
Sarah Vigers

Mediating International Child Abduction Cases

The Hague Convention

Sarah Vigers

·HART·
PUBLISHING

OXFORD AND PORTLAND, OREGON
2011

Published in the United Kingdom by Hart Publishing Ltd
16C Worcester Place, Oxford, OX1 2JW
Telephone: +44 (0)1865 517530
Fax: +44 (0)1865 510710
E-mail: mail@hartpub.co.uk
Website: http://www.hartpub.co.uk

Published in North America (US and Canada) by
Hart Publishing
c/o International Specialized Book Services
920 NE 58th Avenue, Suite 300
Portland, OR 97213-3786
USA
Tel: +1 503 287 3093 or toll-free: (1) 800 944 6190
Fax: +1 503 280 8832
E-mail: orders@isbs.com
Website: http://www.isbs.com

British Library Cataloguing in Publication Data
Data Available

ISBN: 978-1-84946-181-8

Typeset by Hope Services, Abingdon

To my parents, with thanks for always seeing the best in me

SERIES EDITORS' PREFACE

Sarah Vigers is known in the private international law of family law community, by some by her maiden name of Armstrong, partly because of her work for a number of years as a lawyer in the Permanent Bureau of the Hague Conference on Private International Law. Indeed, one of her major accomplishments in the Permanent Bureau was to be the author of a Note on the Development of cross-border family mediation for children particularly in the context of the 1980 Hague Child Abduction Convention (Preliminary Document No 5/2006, see chapter 1, note 5). It was a great pleasure for the School of Law at the University of Aberdeen that she then chose to undertake an LLM by research under the supervision of Paul Beaumont that took as its theme mediation in Hague Child Abduction cases. This gave Sarah the opportunity to build on her excellent work at The Hague with further empirical and library-based research. She also took the opportunity to become qualified as a mediator in family law matters in Scotland and to gain useful experience as a mediator in a range of cases. She was awarded her LLM by research with Distinction on the recommendation of the examiners, including Professor David McClean, who also recommended the thesis for publication in this Series as a short book.

The book addresses three key questions in chapters two to four: what is Convention mediation; how can a mediation process fit within the urgent time constraints of the Convention and its regional application in the EU; and why offer mediation in Convention cases? The author beautifully delineates the type of mediation that can work in the context of the Convention and explains its added value over court proceedings. One added value is, as always with mediation, that it may make the situation less confrontational than it would be if court proceedings were used. Perhaps the key reason, however, is that it gives the mediator the opportunity to enable the parties to settle the merits of the custody dispute in a way that is not possible in return proceedings in an abduction case where the judges are expressly barred from dealing with the merits of the custody dispute.

The book has a resonance for child abduction cases that are resolved in the courts rather than by mediation because of the excellent chapter on the voice of the child in child abduction cases. It is sensitive to the risk that systematically hearing children of almost all ages in child abduction cases might be harmful for the children and therefore not in their best interests, despite them having a right to be heard.

Overall this is a short but beautifully crafted book. It is of relevance, and should be enlightening, to anyone with an interest in the Hague Child Abduction Convention and to all those who care about cross-border family mediation.

Hopefully the very well thought through ideas about how Convention mediation should operate in practice will enable many more Contracting States to the Hague Child Abduction Convention to invest sufficient resources in mediation to make it happen and reduce the expensive burden on the taxpayer of legal aid for return proceedings in the courts.

Paul R Beaumont (University of Aberdeen)
Jonathan Harris (King's College, London)

ACKNOWLEDGEMENTS

I am indebted to my thesis supervisor Professor Paul Beaumont at Aberdeen Law School for his wisdom and patience during the writing of my thesis. I am also grateful to the Permanent Bureau of the Hague Conference on Private International Law for its support over several years, and to Counselling and Family Mediation Grampian for the many opportunities that have been afforded to me in my work as a Family Mediator.

I would particularly like to express my appreciation to all the authorities and individuals who have aided this research by way of responding to my questionnaire, replying to email requests and meeting with me in person or by telephone. Without their expertise and their perspectives from different areas of the globe, it would not have been possible to complete this work.

On a personal level I would like to thank my husband Brad, whose constant love, support and humour ensure that life is never dull and work is never consuming.

TABLE OF CONTENTS

TABLE OF CASES

European Court of Human Rights

Domestic Case Law

TABLE OF LEGISLATION

Domestic Legislation and Regulation

1

Introduction

I. Aim and Purpose

There is growing enthusiasm for the use of mediation to seek to resolve cases arising under the Hague Convention of 25 October 1980 on the Civil Aspects of International Child Abduction (the Convention).[1] However, despite being endorsed by the conclusions of meetings of experts,[2] judicial comment[3] and even legislative changes,[4] there have been relatively few cases where mediation has played a significant role.[5] It is suggested that the reason underlying this dichotomy

* This book is based on a thesis entitled, 'From Enthusiasm to Action: Mediating Return Applications Arising Under the Hague Child Abduction Convention' which was written in 2008/09 and submitted for the award of LLM at the University of Aberdeen, United Kingdom.

[1] Convention on the Civil Aspects of International Child Abduction (adopted 25 October 1980, entered into force 1 December 1983) 1343 UNTS 89 [The Convention].

[2] eg 'Conclusions and Recommendations of the Fifth Meeting of the Special Commission to Review the Operation of the Hague Convention of 25 October 1980 on the Civil Aspects of International Child Abduction and the Practical Implementation of the Hague Convention of 19 October 1996 on Jurisdiction, Applicable Law, Recognition, Enforcement and Co-operation in respect of Parental Responsibility and Measures for the Protection of Children (October–November 2006) www.hcch.net/upload/concl28sc5_e.pdf [2006 Conclusions].

[3] eg *Re H and Others (Minors) (Abduction: Acquiescence)* [1998] AC 72 quoting Waite LJ [footnote]: 'the role in these international cases of priest and mullah, mediator and elder, can often be invaluable in bringing about through parental conciliation the harmony in the lives of children which it is the express purpose of the Convention to achieve'.

[4] Arrêté fédéral portant mise en œuvre des conventions sur l'enlèvement international d'enfants et portant approbation et mise en œuvre des Conventions de La Haye sur la protection des enfants et des adultes du 21 décembre 2007, Feuille Fédérale No 1 (2008) 33–40 RS 211.222.32 www.admin.ch/ch/f/ff/2008/33.pdf [Swiss legislation]. For discussion see A Bucher, 'The New Swiss Federal Act on International Child Abduction' (2008) 4 *Journal of Private International Law* 139 [Bucher 2008]; A Bucher, 'l'intérêt de l'enfant pénètre la convention sur l'enlèvement' in *Vers de nouveaux équilibres entre ordres juridiques, Liber amicorum Hélène Gaudemet-Tallon*, (Paris, Dalloz, 2008) 683. In February 2009 the Ministry of Justice of Serbia formed a working group to draft a new law implementing the Convention which will 'include provisions supporting the use of mediation in child abduction cases where appropriate', J Arsić , 'Family Mediation Concerning Couples of Different Ethnic Origin in the Region of the Former Yugoslavia' [Arsić 2009] (7th European Conference on Family Law on International Family Mediation, Strasbourg, France, March 2009) www.coe.int/t/e/legal_affairs/legal_cooperation/family_law_and_children's_rights/Conferences/7th%20European%20Conference%20on%20Family%20Law%20on%20international%20family%20mediation.asp [2009 Strasbourg Conference].

[5] S Vigers, 'Note on the Development of Mediation, Conciliation and Similar Means to Facilitate Agreed Solutions in Transfrontier Family Disputes Concerning Children especially in the context of the Hague Convention of 1980' Prel. Doc. No 5/2006 http://hcch.e-vision.nl/upload/wop/abd_pd05e2006.pdf [Note on the Development of Mediation]. Interestingly, there has been little progress in terms of new initiatives since this document was drafted.

between the widespread support for the use of mediation and the current limited practice is that there are several key questions regarding the use of mediation in the context of the Convention which remain to be answered. Specifically: What is meant by Convention mediation? How can a mediation process fit within the constraints of the Convention? And why offer mediation in Convention cases given the existing legal framework? This book aims to address these preliminary questions and in so doing to encourage a movement from enthusiasm about the use of mediation in the Convention context, to greater practice.

Discussion of mediation in the context of the Convention is timely. Some notable initiatives are taking place and several States have expressed intention to (further) develop mediation in the Convention context.[6] As a result of increased discussion and action in the field, the topic was placed on the agenda of the meeting of the fifth Special Commission to review the operation of the instrument held in 2006.[7] A preliminary document was prepared on the subject[8] and a half-day set aside for discussion. This meeting welcomed the 'mediation initiatives and projects which are taking place in Contracting States'[9] and invited the Permanent Bureau of the Hague Conference on Private International Law (Permanent Bureau) to 'continue to keep States informed of developments in the mediation of cross-border disputes concerning contact and abduction'.[10] Furthermore, in 2008 the Council of the Hague Conference asked the Permanent Bureau to prepare a Guide to Good Practice on the use of mediation in the context of the Convention,[11] to be submitted for consideration at the next meeting of the Special Commission, which is likely to be held in 2011.[12]

The development of Convention mediation has also been the subject of discussion at other international conferences.[13] Additionally, other international and

[6] ibid.

[7] Convened by the Secretary General of the Hague Conference, a Special Commission meeting to review the practical operation of the Convention takes place every four or five years. There have been five such meetings, held in October 1989, January 1993, March 1997, March 2001 and October/November 2006. Additionally, there was a specific Special Commission held in September 2002 to review the first two parts of the Guide to Good Practice. Special Commission meetings involve experts from Members of the Hague Conference; States Parties to the relevant Convention and invited international governmental and non-governmental organisations.

[8] Note on the Development of Mediation (n 5).

[9] 2006 Conclusions (n 2) [1.3.2].

[10] ibid [1.3.3].

[11] The Permanent Bureau has established a Group of Experts to assist with the development of this Guide to Good Practice. There are four published parts of the Guide to Good Practice: *Part I on Central Authority Practice* (Bristol, Family Law, 2003); *Part II on Implementing Measures* (Bristol, Family Law, 2003) [Guide on Implementing Measures]; *Part III on Preventive Measures* (Bristol, Family Law, 2005) [Guide on Preventive Measures]; *General Principles and Guide to Good Practice on Transfrontier Contact Concerning Children* (Bristol, Family Law, 2008) [Guide on Transfrontier Contact] www.hcch.net/index_en.php?act=text.display&tid=21#gpg.

[12] 'Conclusions and Recommendations of the Council on General Affairs and Policy of the Conference' (April 2008) www.hcch.net/upload/wop/genaff_concl08e.pdf [2008 Conclusions].

[13] 'Cross-Border Family Mediation with an Emphasis on the 1980 Hague Convention on the Civil Aspects of International Child Abduction' (University of Miami, School of Law, 22–24 February 2008) www.law.miami.edu/cle/pdf/Mediation_Training_Feb2208_v3.pdf. Some of the papers presented at this conference have been published in (2008) 40 *University of Miami Inter-American Law Review*. The

regional family law instruments specifically advocate for the promotion of mediation and some of these interact with the application of the Convention, notably the Hague Convention on Jurisdiction, Applicable Law, Recognition, Enforcement and Co-operation in respect of Parental Responsibility and Measures for the Protection of Children (the 1996 Hague Convention)[14] and Council Regulation (EC) 2201/2003 of 27 November 2003 concerning jurisdiction and the recognition and enforcement of judgments in matrimonial matters and the matters of parental responsibility, repealing Regulation (EC) No 1347/2000 [2003] (the Brussels II *bis* Regulation).[15] The use of mediation to handle Convention cases is also specifically endorsed in the Practice Guide to the Brussels II *bis* Regulation.[16] There is thus impetus to move forward and the time is ripe to seek to contribute to the discussion, with the aim of informing further development.

The primary purpose of this book is to offer a response to some of the perceived barriers to the use of mediation in the Convention context. However, analysing the use of mediation in the context of the Convention has important broader implications. Firstly, it is recognised that mediation or similar processes are particularly useful where the Convention is not applicable,[17] either because the instrument is not in force between the relevant States or because the factual circumstances of the case fall outside the instrument's scope. Focus is on Convention applications as these sit within a firm legal framework which forms the backdrop to mediation and offers a context within which to assess the usefulness of the discipline. However, mechanisms established for the purposes of Convention mediation could potentially be adapted to provide a process to handle these cases which might otherwise fall outside an adequate framework and where mediation may be particularly useful.[18]

Secondly, discussion of Convention mediation will influence the development of cross-border family mediation more generally. This subject is being discussed within several international and regional organisations including the Council of

author is grateful to Jennifer Zawid for providing a copy of her article. In October 2008 there was a session on 'mediation in international child abduction cases' at the International Bar Association's annual conference www.int-bar.org/images/downloads/confs/finalprog.pdf.

[14] Convention on Jurisdiction, Applicable Law, Recognition, Enforcement and Co-operation in respect of Parental Responsibility and Measures for the Protection of Children (adopted 19 October 1996, entered into force 1 January 2002) 35 ILM 1391 [1996 Hague Convention] Art 31.

[15] Council Regulation (EC) 2201/2003 of 27 November 2003 concerning jurisdiction and the recognition and enforcement of judgments in matrimonial matters and the matters of parental responsibility, repealing Regulation (EC) No 1347/2000 [2003] OJ338/2 [Brussels II *bis* Regulation] Art 55.

[16] 'Practice Guide for the application of the new Brussels II Regulation' http://ec.europa.eu/justice_home/doc_centre/civil/doc/parental_resp_ec_vdm_en.pdf [Practice Guide].

[17] See the non-Convention case of *Al-Khatib v Masry* [2004] EWCA 1353 per Thorpe LJ [17]: '[t]here is no case, however conflicted, which is not potentially open to successful mediation' [*Al-Khatib* [2004]].

[18] Third Malta Judicial Conference on Cross-Frontier Family Law Issues, hosted by the Government of Malta in collaboration with the Hague Conference on Private International Law www.hcch.net/upload/maltadecl09_e.pdf [Malta Declaration] [7]. Additionally, the Permanent Bureau has established a Working Party on mediation in the context of the Malta Process www.hcch.net/index_en?act=progress.listing&cat=7.

Europe,[19] the European Union[20] and the Hague Conference.[21] Members of the latter organisation have expressly decided to follow developments primarily in relation to the use of mediation in the Convention context before proceeding to more formal debate on the broader subject.[22] Indeed although practice is limited in the Convention context there is more experience of cross-border family mediation in this specific area than in the broader field.[23] The importance of the subject matter of this book therefore goes beyond the immediate context and may act as a catalyst for the further development of cross-border family mediation more generally.

II. Structure and Scope

As there is currently little practice of Convention mediation it was not possible to undertake detailed empirical work. However, a Questionnaire was sent to 60 Central Authorities and to a number of other experts in the field, including mediators and judges.[24] This Questionnaire is attached as an appendix. A series of meetings was also held in person and by telephone with a view to gaining contemporaneous information on the current situation in different Contracting States,

[19] 2009 Strasbourg Conference (n 4).

[20] Code of Conduct for Mediators (Brussels, July 2004) [European Code of Conduct]; Directive 2008/52/EC of the European Parliament and of the Council of 21 May 2008 on certain aspects of mediation in civil and commercial matters [Mediation Directive]; the transposition date is 21 May 2011.

[21] In 2006 the Permanent Bureau was asked to draw up a Feasibility Study on Cross Border Mediation in Family Matters, 'Conclusions of the Special Commission of 3 – 5 April 2006 on General Affairs and Policy of the Conference' www.hcch.net/upload/wop/genaff_pd11e2007.pdf. This Study was presented to Members in 2007: 'Feasibility Study on Cross-Border Mediation in Family Matters' Prel. Doc. No 20/2007 www.hcch.net/upload/wop/genaff_pd20e2007.pdf [2007 Feasibility Study].

[22] 2008 Conclusions (n 12).

[23] Council of Europe Working Group on Mediation, 'Analysis on assessment of the impact of Council of Europe recommendations concerning mediation' CEPEJ (2007) 12 (Strasbourg, 3 May 2007) 61. Only two respondent States had specific mechanisms for international mediation both of which were in the child abduction context.

[24] The Questionnaire was distributed from May 2008. Responses are on file with the author [Questionnaire Responses]. To gain a broad overview the Questionnaire was sent to all Central Authorities which have published an email address. The author is grateful to the following Central Authorities for their responses: Argentina, Australia, Austria, Belgium, Canada, China (Hong Kong Special Administrative Region), Denmark, England and Wales, Finland, France, Germany, Italy, Malta, Monaco, Montserrat, New Zealand, Norway, Poland, Portugal, Scotland, Slovenia, South Africa, Sweden, Switzerland, United States of America. The author would also like to thank the following individuals and organisations: Judge Peter Boshier (New Zealand), Judge Eberhard Carl (Germany), Ms Denise Carter (reunite – International Child Abduction Centre), Judge Martina Erb-Klünemann (Germany), Ms Lorraine Filion (*Association internationale francophone des intervenants auprès des familles séparées* (AIFI)), Judge Annette Olland (Netherlands), Judge Astrid Schwichtenberg (Germany), Judge Øyvind Smukkestad (Norway), Lord Justice Mathew Thorpe (England and Wales), Mr Christoph Paul and Ms Sybille Kiesewetter (German Federal Association of Family Mediators (BAFM)), Ms Helga Krueger-Pompl, Ms Alison Hulstine, Ms Tessa Lehman and Ms Felicitas Lauer (American Consulate in Germany), International Social Service (ISS) (German and Swiss Branches).

and views on how Convention mediation might further develop.[25] Two other sources in particular deserve prominent mention: firstly, responses to questionnaires sent out by the Permanent Bureau of the Hague Conference;[26] and, secondly, the report of a mediation pilot project undertaken by reunite – International Child Abduction Centre in England, which details the only current empirical research on mediation in the context of the Convention.[27]

Drawing from this research it is submitted that there are three broad questions which require to be answered if Convention mediation is to be used more widely: What is Convention mediation? How can a mediation process fit within the constraints of the Convention? And, why offer mediation in Convention cases? Each of the first three substantive chapters seeks to respond to one of these questions. As the use of mediation in the Convention context remains novel in most States these questions are intentionally broad with the aim of providing an overview of how the mediation process can operate in the Convention context.

Chapter two answers the question, 'what is Convention mediation?' Firstly, by distinguishing mediation from other processes and proposing a working description. Secondly, by explaining the mediation process and outlining its place within the procedure for handling a Convention application. Devoting an entire chapter to issues that might be considered merely introductory is justified because there is widespread confusion surrounding terminology and practice,[28] which if left unaddressed could hinder the development of Convention mediation and cross-border mediation more generally.

The third chapter addresses the question, 'how can a mediation process fit within the constraints of the Convention?' As Convention mediation is significantly different to domestic (and even more general cross-border) family mediation it is suggested in the first part of the chapter that it should be viewed as a distinct discipline. The second part of the chapter highlights specific legal, procedural and practical challenges raised by mediating in Convention cases which illustrate the advantages of this approach. These issues are intentionally discussed broadly as at this early stage of development a broad general overview was considered important. It is assumed that many of these issues are likely to form the basis of the Guide to Good Practice.[29]

[25] The author is grateful to: Ms Julia Alanen (23 April 2009); Justice Victoria Bennett (1 December 2008); Judge Eberhard Carl (24 June 2008); Ms Denise Carter (19 September 2008 and 4-5 December 2008) and the team at reunite (4–5 December 2008); Mr Doug Frenkel (17 April 2009); Ms Lisa Parkinson (12 January 2009); Lord Justice Mathew Thorpe (24 November 2008); Ms Jennifer Zawid (19 and 23 September 2008); and to Mr Ignacio Goicoechea and Ms Melissa Kucinski.

[26] 'Collated Responses to the Questionnaire concerning the Practical Operation of the Hague Convention of 25 October 1980 on the Civil Aspects of International Child Abduction' Prel. Doc. No 2/2006 http://hcch.e-vision.nl/upload/wop/abd_pd02efs2006.pdf [2006 Responses]; 'Feasibility Study on Cross-border Mediation in Family Matters – Responses to the Questionnaire' Prel. Doc. No 10/2008 www.hcch.net/upload/wop/genaff_pd10_2008.pdf [Feasibility Study Responses].

[27] reunite, 'Mediation in International Parental Child Abduction: The reunite Mediation Pilot Scheme' (October 2006) www.reunite.org/edit/files/Mediation%20Report.pdf [reunite Report].

[28] 2006 Responses (n 26) 44–54, 264–89.

[29] n 11.

Chapter four responds to the question, 'why offer mediation in Convention cases?' This chapter primarily focuses on the fact that mediation has the potential to address many of the concerns regarding the operation of the Convention in the present day. The second and smaller part of the chapter examines additional wider benefits offered by mediation as opposed to court-based solutions.

The final substantive chapter focuses on the voice of the child. This issue has been chosen for more detailed discussion for three reasons. Firstly, there have been some interesting dicta in recent Convention cases outlining the changing role of the voice of the child in court proceedings, which has implications for hearing the child in mediation. Secondly, the suggested approach to the voice of the child in Convention mediation serves as an illustration of how mediation is viewed in this book. Thirdly, it is a subject which has not been discussed in any detail elsewhere.

The general scope of this book is further limited in two broad respects. Firstly, discussion is restricted to mediation in the context of handling return applications. Consequently, the issue of mediating applications for contact is not directly addressed. The rationale for this omission is, firstly, because there are specific challenges to mediation raised by the return mechanism which require discussion. Secondly, because the Convention provides a specific and distinct legal framework for return applications within which mediation must operate and against which analysis and evaluation can therefore take place. Conversely, with regard to applications for contact the only substantive provision is interpreted differently in different States such that in some States contact applications are handled under the instrument while in other States they fall to be resolved under domestic law.[30] The consequent absence of a coherent legal framework to support cross-border contact under the Convention makes the development of mediation in these cases more vulnerable.[31] It is therefore proposed that pioneering mediation in the context of applications for return is a better first step, which it is hoped will lead to further discussion and development of mediation to handle applications for contact, where mediation may be particularly useful.

Secondly, the scope of this book is restricted to the use of mediation to handle applications arising under the Convention. Mediation at a domestic level has value in preventing abduction,[32] enforcing orders[33] and dealing with the substantive issues of the dispute after a Convention application has been dealt with. The

[30] Art 21. For detailed analysis see W Duncan, 'Transfrontier Access/Contact General Principles and Good Practice' Prel. Doc. No 4/2006 http://hcch.e-vision.nl/upload/wop/abd_pd04e2006.pdf [Duncan 2006] and Guide on Transfrontier Contact (n 11).

[31] However, the development of mediation to resolve return cases could be a useful first step towards the development of cross-border mediation to resolve contact cases, see ch 4, III.C.

[32] Guide on Preventive Measures (n 11) 15–16. In Quebec, Canada mediators requested and were given special training on the Convention to assist them in working with couples in Canada where abduction was a threat, 2006 Responses (n 26) 284–9.

[33] A Schulz, 'Enforcement of Orders made under the 1980 Convention – A Comparative Legal Study' Prel. Doc. No 6/2006 http://hcch.e-vision.nl/upload/wop/abd_pd06e2006.pdf; A Schulz, 'Enforcement of Orders made under the 1980 Convention – Towards Principles of Good Practice' Prel. Doc. No 7/2006 http://hcch.e-vision.nl/upload/wop/abd_pd07e2006.pdf [Enforcement Reports].

further development of mediation at a domestic level will have a positive impact on the operation of Convention mediation but is not discussed.

III. Background and Context

The stated aims of the Convention are found in Article 1:

> to secure the prompt return of children wrongfully removed to or retained in any Contracting State and to ensure that rights of custody or of access under the law of one Contracting State are effectively respected in the other Contracting States.

For the Convention to apply the child in question must be under 16 and have been habitually resident in a Contracting State prior to the removal or retention.[34] The Convention must be in force between the relevant Contracting States[35] and the removal or retention must be 'wrongful', that is in breach of rights of custody which were being exercised prior to the abduction.[36] Each Contracting State is required to designate a Central Authority 'to discharge the duties which are imposed by the Convention'.[37] Where less than one year has elapsed between the date of the wrongful removal or retention and the commencement of proceedings in the State of refuge, the judicial or administrative authorities must order the return of the child forthwith,[38] unless one of the exceptions is made out.[39]

The exceptions are listed exhaustively in Articles 12, 13 and 20 and where an Article 13 exception is made out the authorities have discretion nevertheless to order return.[40] Exceptions are intended to be applied narrowly,[41] and to a large extent judges in Contracting States have upheld a strict interpretation, such that in the majority of litigated cases the court orders the return of the child. Two

[34] Art 4.

[35] All Member States of the Hague Conference at the time of its Fourteenth Session are entitled to ratify the Convention (Art 37), and any other State may accede (Art 38). The Convention enters into force for a Contracting State on the first day of the third calendar month following the deposit of its instrument of ratification or accession (Art 43). A State which ratifies the Convention has treaty relations with every other ratifying State from the moment the Convention enters into force for that State. However, where a State accedes to the Convention existing Contracting States have to declare their acceptance of the accession and treaty relations commence on the first day of the third calendar month following the deposit of the declaration of acceptance (Art 38). As a result of this procedure not all Contracting States enjoy treaty relations with each other.

[36] Rights of custody may 'arise in particular by operation of law or by reason of a judicial or administrative decision, or by reason of an agreement having legal effect under the law of that State' (Art 3). 'Rights of custody shall include rights relating to the care of the person of the child and, in particular, the right to determine the child's place of residence' (Art 5a).

[37] Art 6.

[38] Art 12.

[39] Arts 12, 13 and 20.

[40] Arts 13 and 18.

[41] E Pérez-Vera, 'Explanatory Report' in *Actes et documents de la quatorzième session, Tome III, Enlèvement d'enfants* (Hague Conference, The Hague, 1982) 426 [Explanatory Report] [34], [Actes et documents 1982].

global studies of cases commenced in 1999 and 2003 revealed that in the respective years 74 per cent and 79 per cent of cases going to court resulted in a return order being made.[42] The Convention is premised on the notion that the *status quo* should be restored to enable the authorities in the State of habitual residence to make any necessary orders in relation to the substantive issues of the dispute, in the best interests of the child.[43] Thus speed is important to minimise disruption and to this end Contracting States are mandated to use the most expeditious procedures available and authorities can be asked to account for any delay of longer than six weeks.[44]

The Convention is widely deemed to be an enduring and successful instrument which has stood the test of time. 30 years after it was drafted it continues to attract new States, and with currently 84 Contracting States,[45] it is one of the most adhered to Hague Conventions.[46] Significantly, 60 per cent of Contracting States were not Members of the Hague Conference at the time the Convention was drafted,[47] demonstrating that its appeal goes far beyond the traditional Hague community. The Convention has been declared compatible with national constitutions,[48] and human rights instruments, notably the United Nations Convention on the Rights of the Child (United Nations Convention)[49] and the European Convention for the Protection of Human Rights and Fundamental Freedoms (European Convention).[50] Additionally, the Convention withstood a

[42] N Lowe, S Armstrong and A Mathias 'A Statistical Analysis of Applications made in 1999 under the Hague Convention of 25 October 1980 on the Civil Aspects of International Child Abduction' Prel. Doc. No 3/2001 (Revised version, November 2001) http://hcch.e-vision.nl/upload/abd2001pd3e.pdf [1999 Study]; N Lowe, 'A Statistical Analysis of Applications made in 2003 under the Hague Convention of 25 October 1980 on the Civil Aspects of International Child Abduction: Part I: Overall Report' Prel. Doc. No 3/2006 (2007 update) http://hcch.e-vision.nl/upload/wop/abd_pd03e1_2007.pdf 2008 [2003 Study].

[43] Explanatory Report (n 41) [16].

[44] Arts 2 and 11.

[45] Since 2006 the following States have ratified or acceded to the Convention: San Marino (2006); Ukraine (2006); Albania (2007); The Seychelles (2008); Morocco (2010); Gabon (2010) and Singapore (2010). For up to date information on the number of Contracting States see www.hcch.net/index_en.php?act=conventions.status&cid=24.

[46] At the time of writing the Convention is the second most adhered to Hague Convention behind the Convention Abolishing the Requirement of Legalisation for Foreign Public Documents (adopted 5 October 1961, entered into force 24 January 1965) 527 UNTS 189 which had 99 Contracting States (at 1 January 2011).

[47] Over half of these States have gone on to become Members of the Hague Conference, while 27 per cent of all Contracting States remain non-Members of the Organisation.

[48] For an overview see W Duncan, 'Action In Support of the Hague Child Abduction Convention: A View from the Permanent Bureau' (2000) 33 *New York University Journal of International Law & Politics* 103, 122.

[49] Convention on the Rights of the Child (adopted 20 November 1989, entered into force 2 September 1990) 1577 UNTS 3 [United Nations Convention]. The Committee on the Rights of the Child has encouraged States Parties to ratify the Hague Convention as a way of fulfilling their obligations under Art 11 [General Observations No 5 (2003)].

[50] Convention for the Protection of Human Rights and Fundamental Freedoms (adopted 4 November 1950, entered into force 3 September 1953) ETS No 5 [European Convention]. The European Court of Human Rights has held that the positive obligations flowing from Art 8 of the European Convention regarding reuniting a parent and a child must be interpreted in the light of the Hague Convention. See, inter alia, *Ignaccolo-Zenide v Romania* [2000] ECtHR no 31679/96. For

challenge from the European Community which ultimately opted to maintain the Convention regime, albeit with the addition of certain elements to be applied in the intra-European Union context.[51] Importantly, the Contracting States to the Convention have also acknowledged that it is generally functioning well and meeting the needs for which it was drafted.[52] Indeed the Convention 'remains an extremely valuable instrument', which is 'alive, well and capable of living in the twenty-first century world community'.[53]

Notwithstanding this widespread support there are a number of concerns regarding the operation of the Convention in the present day. Discussion of Convention mediation must take place cognisant of these concerns and conscious of the fact that abduction is not merely a legal problem but it also has a human face. If Convention mediation is to add value to the current Convention regime it must offer some additional advantage to the parties, and the child. Concerns regarding the operation of the instrument largely stem from the fact that the Convention essentially envisages a two-step process. First there is the Convention case, which effectively establishes the correct forum for the second case on the substantive issues of the dispute. The principal advantage of Convention mediation is that parties in mediation are free to devise their own solutions and are not restricted to the application of the relevant law. They can thus negotiate the place of the child's residence in one-step, taking account of relevant substantive issues. If mediation can address real and important concerns it could add great value to the current regime.

IV. Conclusion

While it is generally acknowledged that mediation could add value to the current Convention regime, there is little established practice as questions remain to be answered. This book seeks to offer some response to these questions in the hope of encouraging a movement from enthusiasm about mediation to a greater use of the discipline.

discussion see P Beaumont, 'European Court of Human Rights Cases Concerning The Hague Convention on International Child Abduction' in *The Jurisprudence of the European Court of Human Rights and the European Court of Justice on the Hague Convention on International Child Abduction* (Leiden, Martinus Nijhoff Publishers, 2009) [Beaumont 2009].

[51] Brussels II *bis* Regulation (n 14) Art 60 and Recital 17. The Regulation applies in all intra-European Union cases (except those involving Denmark, Art 2(3)). For analysis of the interaction between the Convention and the Brussels II *bis* Regulation see D Hodson, *A Practical Guide to International Family Law* (Wiltshire, Family Law, 2008) 269–75.

[52] 'Conclusions and Recommendations of the Fourth Meeting of the Special Commission to Review the Operation of the Hague Convention of 25 October 1980 on the Civil Aspects of International Child Abduction' (March 2001) http://hcch.evision.nl/upload/concl28sc4_e.pdf [2001 Conclusions].

[53] M Freeman and H Setright, 'The Hague Child Abduction Convention: Current Developments in Hague Convention Jurisprudence or a Universal Vaccine for a Mutating Virus?' [2002 2003] 6 *Contemporary Issues in Law* 279, 279–80.

2

What is Convention Mediation?

I. Introduction

To promote a greater use of mediation in the context of the Convention it is vital to ensure that there is a clear understanding of what mediation is and how it fits within the broader procedure for handling a Convention application. Even a cursory glance at documentation pertaining to mediation in the context of the Convention reveals that the notion has been construed in different ways and is not well understood.[1] This has led to a certain amount of discussion proceeding at cross-purposes and if left unaddressed could hinder the development of Convention mediation. Additionally, it is clear that the place of mediation within the context of the broader procedure for handling a Convention application is differently conceived, leading to different understandings of the aim and purpose of mediation. This chapter seeks to offer some clarity as to what mediation is and how it fits within the procedure for handling a Convention application.

The opening part of this chapter addresses definitional disparities by drawing a distinction between 'mediation' and other recognised forms of assisted dispute resolution; and by distinguishing 'mediation' from the Convention concepts of 'voluntary return' and 'amicable resolution'.[2] This part of the chapter concludes with a proposed working description and an explanation of the mediation process. The second part focuses on the place of mediation within the broader procedure for handling a Convention application. In this regard it is suggested that mediation should be viewed generally as one aspect of this broader procedure; and specifically as an alternative to the court hearing.

[1] 'Collated Responses to the Questionnaire concerning the Practical Operation of the Hague Convention of 25 October 1980 on the Civil Aspects of International Child Abduction' Prel. Doc. No 2/2006 http://hcch.e-vision.nl/upload/wop/abd_pd02efs2006.pdf [2006 Responses] 44–54, 264–89.

[2] Convention on the Civil Aspects of International Child Abduction (adopted 25 October 1980, entered into force 1 December 1983) 1343 UNTS 89, Arts 7(2)(c) and 10.

II. Definitional Difficulties

A. Distinguishing Mediation from Other Forms of Assisted Dispute Resolution

'Mediation' is a well-used term and is thus considered to be well understood. However, it has a broad range of meanings in a multiplicity of contexts such that the term is often used with a lack of precision. Mediation can describe, inter alia, diplomacy between States, negotiation in times of war or hostage situations, and conflict resolution between natural or legal persons in a variety of civil, commercial and family settings. Even within the narrow context of family mediation it is used simultaneously as an umbrella term to describe almost any process which promotes agreement between the parties with the assistance of a third party, and narrowly to refer to a specific technical process.[3]

Three forms of assisted dispute resolution are common in family matters: informal negotiations; the court process; and formal non-adversarial processes. Informal negotiations involve the assistance of a third person who does not necessarily have any specific training and who does not attempt to follow a recognised process. These negotiations may even exclude one of the parties to the dispute; instead the third party may seek to persuade one party to alter his position. In the Convention context this is akin to the procedure in many States for seeking voluntary return or amicable resolution. Often Central Authorities write to, or organise a meeting with, abductors. The Central Authority explains the Convention to the abductor and seeks to encourage him or her to return the child. These letters or discussions are very important in Convention cases and can lead to the abductor voluntarily returning the child.

Secondly, many family disputes are resolved through the court process. This may involve litigation and adjudication or, very often, negotiated solutions falling short of formal adjudication. These negotiations are usually led by judges or lawyers and are also common in Convention cases, often leading to consent orders. In the study of cases commenced in 1999 consent orders were not viewed as an outcome in their own right but were usually included within the categorisation of judicial return orders. The significance of consent orders was however realised and the study of cases commenced in 2003 included consent orders as

[3] 'The lack of [a] substantial distinction has meant that the word mediation is used almost as a synonym of alternative dispute resolution and with this term all such processes are included such as conciliation, facilitation or arbitration without obligatory award, etc..' D Bustelo, 'Family Mediation in Ibero-America' (7th European Conference on Family Law on International Family Mediation, Strasbourg, France, March 2009) www.coe.int/t/e/legal_affairs/legal_cooperation/family_law_and_children's_rights/Conferences/7th%20European%20Conference%20on%20Family%20Law%20on%20international%20family%20mediation.asp [2009 Strasbourg Conference].

an independent outcome. Globally 9 per cent of applications resulted in this outcome.[4]

The third and final common form of assisted dispute resolution is formal non-adversarial processes. These involve a trained third person who uses a prescribed approach to assist the parties to resolve their own dispute. The most usual processes in family matters are mediation, conciliation and, more recently, collaborative law. These latter processes are as yet not well used in the Convention context. However, it is mediation in this context which is the subject of this book.

All of the three types of assisted dispute resolution described above, with the exception of litigation and adjudication which does not lead to a consent order, might be termed 'mediation' depending upon who is formulating the definition. Certainly in the Convention context several different processes falling into each of the above categories have been referred to as 'mediation'.[5] In part this confusion is to be expected because the broader subject of cross-border family mediation has not yet fully developed either as a term or as a practice. Thus the development of Convention mediation is not a matter of adapting and refining an existing practice to fit the specific circumstances of the instrument. Rather it is a case of pioneering the practice within the specific context of the Convention without the benefit of definitional clarity flowing from experience in the more general field.

Additionally, focus to date in the cross-border context has tended to rest on facilitating agreements rather than on the particular processes through which this might be achieved. To this end cross-border instruments generally favour a non-exhaustive list of options, including, 'mediation', 'conciliation', 'similar' or 'other' 'means' or 'processes'.[6] There is certainly benefit in discussing facilitation of agreement in family matters in the broadest possible sense allowing States to use whatever processes are available for the purpose of promoting agreement and protecting the child. However, it is suggested that the time is also ripe to seek to further develop particular processes in the cross-border, and specifically the Convention, context. To do so it is necessary to distinguish between them. For the purposes of this book 'mediation' is therefore used to refer to a particular process practised by persons qualified as mediators. Thus the first definitional distinction is made between mediation as a specific process and other recognised forms of dispute resolution, many of which play a very important role in Convention applications.

[4] N Lowe, 'A Statistical Analysis of Applications made in 2003 under the Hague Convention of 25 October 1980 on the Civil Aspects of International Child Abduction: Part I: Overall Report' Prel. Doc. No 3/2006 (2007 update) http://hcch.e-vision.nl/upload/wop/abd_pd03e1_2007.pdf [2003 Study] 30.

[5] 2006 Responses (n 1) 264–89.

[6] eg Convention on Jurisdiction, Applicable Law, Recognition, Enforcement and Co-operation in respect of Parental Responsibility and Measures for the Protection of Children (adopted 19 October 1996, entered into force 1 January 2002) 35 ILM 1391 [1996 Hague Convention] Art 31; Council Regulation (EC) 2201/2003 of 27 November 2003 concerning jurisdiction and the recognition and enforcement of judgments in matrimonial matters and the matters of parental responsibility, repealing Regulation (EC) No 1347/2000 [2003] OJ338/2 [Brussels II *bis* Regulation] Art 55 and the Hague Convention on the International Recovery of Child Support and Other Forms of Family Maintenance (concluded 23 November 2007) Arts 6(2)(d) and 34(2)(i).

The primary reason for focusing on mediation as opposed to conciliation or collaborative law is that most practice to date under the Convention has been essentially mediation-based.[7] It is also suggested that mediation is particularly appropriate in these cases.[8] Conciliation suffers from many of the same definitional disparities as mediation and the difference between the two disciplines is not always clear.[9] Thus mediation as here defined may incorporate conciliation.[10] Conversely collaborative law is quite distinct and is not here discussed as the implications for its use differ. The process of four-way meetings raises different issues to the process of mediation and the professionals involved are lawyers not mediators, which also raises different issues. Limiting the scope of this book to the use of mediation is not intended to suggest that other alternative forms of dispute resolution falling outside of mediation are not beneficial in the Convention context. Rather that focusing initially on one technique can address some of the definitional confusion.

B. Distinguishing Mediation from Voluntary Return and Amicable Resolution

The return mechanism is generally and correctly considered to be the heart of the Convention regime; however, it is neither the only nor the primary solution offered by the instrument. The Convention emphasises the importance of 'voluntary return' and 'amicable resolution':

> Central Authorities . . . shall take all appropriate measures . . . to secure the voluntary return of the child or to bring about an amicable resolution of the issues.[11]
>
> The Central Authority of the State where the child is shall take or cause to be taken all appropriate measures in order to obtain the voluntary return of the child.[12]

Seeking voluntary return or amicable resolution is the only duty imposed upon the Central Authorities which is repeated in two separate Articles. This 'highlights the interest of the Convention in seeing parties have recourse to this way of

[7] See S Vigers, 'Note on the Development of Mediation, Conciliation and Similar Means to Facilitate Agreed Solutions in Transfrontier Family Disputes Concerning Children especially in the context of the Hague Convention of 1980' Prel. Doc. No 5/2006 http://hcch.e-vision.nl/upload/wop/abd_pd05e2006.pdf [Note on the Development of Mediation].

[8] See ch 4, III.B.

[9] A difference between conciliation and mediation is that the former is more directive as the conciliator offers advice while the latter is more facilitative. In the Convention context the specific and complex subject matter is likely to require that mediators are at least a little directive and therefore in this context these two disciplines are considered together.

[10] However, a distinction needs to made with the practice in South Africa where 'conciliation' is mandated in each case under the Mediation in Certain Divorce Matters Act (Act 24 of 1987) but refers to negotiations with the abducting parent to seek to secure voluntary return. These negotiations do not involve the other party and are thus not mediation as here defined, Questionnaire Responses (ch 1, n 24) South African Central Authority. See also, R Sherrer and D Louw, 'The Origin and Functioning of the Family Advocate System' (2003) 31 *International Journal of the Sociology of Law* 343.

[11] Art 7.

[12] Art 10.

proceeding'.[13] Indeed the experience of the drafters was that 'a considerable number of cases can be settled without any need to have recourse to the court'.[14] However, despite this intentional emphasis, practice in many Contracting States initially centred on court proceedings and discussion of improving the operation of the Convention tended to focus on improving judicial mechanisms.[15] Given that the Convention was drafted to fill the legal lacuna previously existing in this area, it is not surprising that Contracting States, relying upon the new legal framework, focused their efforts principally on court-based solutions. Indeed efforts to promote voluntary resolution initially developed primarily in relation to cases falling outside the Convention regime, where a legal framework remained absent.[16] Negotiating amicable resolutions was therefore to some extent seen as a solution of last resort where no other solution existed.

Recognition of the value of seeking voluntary return or amicable resolution has, however, undergone a certain renaissance in recent years. This largely reflects the increasing importance placed upon facilitating agreed solutions in the domestic family law of many of the Contracting States. While the subject was little discussed at the three previous meetings of the Special Commission to review the practical operation of the Convention, the fourth meeting, held in 2001, concluded that:

> Contracting States should encourage voluntary return where possible. It is proposed that Central Authorities should as a matter of practice seek to achieve voluntary return, as intended by Article 7 c) of the Convention.[17]

There is some limited evidence that there has been a change in practice. In 18 per cent of all applications in 1999 the child was returned voluntarily, while in 2003 this proportion had risen to 22 per cent.[18] When analysing just those cases which resulted in the return of the child, 36 per cent were resolved by voluntary agreement and 64 per cent by court order in 1999.[19] In 2003 the gap had narrowed considerably to 43 per cent and 57 per cent respectively.[20] While this data only

[13] E Pérez-Vera, 'Explanatory Report' in *Actes et documents de la quatorzième session, Tome III, Enlèvement d'enfants* (Hague Conference, The Hague, 1982) 426 [Explanatory Report] [103].

[14] ibid [92].

[15] See Conclusions and Recommendations of the five Special Commission meetings: www.hcch.net/index_en.php?act=text.display&tid=21#sc [Conclusions of the Special Commissions].

[16] See C Gosselain, 'Child Abduction and Transfrontier Access: Bilateral Conventions and Islamic States: A Research Paper' Prel. Doc. No 7/2002 http://hcch.e-vision.nl/upload/abd2002_pd7e.pdf.

[17] 'Conclusions and Recommendations of the Fourth Meeting of the Special Commission to Review the Operation of the Hague Convention of 25 October 1980 on the Civil Aspects of International Child Abduction' (March 2001) http://hcch.evision.nl/upload/concl28sc4_e.pdf [2001 Conclusions] [1.10].

[18] 2003 Study (n 4) 31.

[19] N Lowe, S Armstrong and A Mathias, 'A Statistical Analysis of Applications made in 1999 under the Hague Convention of 25 October 1980 on the Civil Aspects of International Child Abduction' Prel. Doc. No 3/2001 (Revised version, November 2001) http://hcch.e-vision.nl/upload/abd2001pd3e.pdf [1999 Study] 12.

[20] 2003 Study (n 4) 30.

refers to two years, it is at least noteworthy.[21] A further study is being undertaken by Professor Lowe on cases arising in 2008, which will be presented to the next meeting of the Special Commission likely to be held in 2011. Interestingly, the 2003 Study drew a distinction between 'voluntary returns entirely outside the court and voluntary returns involving judicial consent orders'. The latter were categorised within the number of judicial return orders. Consequently, 'if anything, one may have expected this figure [voluntary returns] to have decreased'.[22] In fact if the judicial consent orders are viewed as voluntary returns the proportion of voluntarily agreed returns increases to 61 per cent.[23]

The 2001 Special Commission also concluded that Central Authorities 'where possible and appropriate' could undertake their obligations under Article 7 of the Convention 'by referral of parties to a specialist organisation providing an appropriate mediation service'. This text is the first explicit reference by a Special Commission to the use of mediation in the Convention context. By the time of the next Special Commission in 2006, mediation was a term, if not a practice, which was well used in relation to the Convention such that it justified its own slot on the agenda. Reference to mediation in the Conclusions of these two Special Commissions in 2001 and 2006 demonstrates that the practice is now accepted by consensus.

It is also generally accepted that although the Convention itself contains no reference to mediation the legal basis for its use stems from the emphasis on voluntary return and amicable resolution. In response to a proposal to enshrine the use of mediation within a Protocol to the Convention, the vast majority of responding States saw no need for any Protocol to provide a legal basis given the existence of Articles 7(2)(c) and 10.[24] A Protocol could, however, assist with detailing some of the practicalities of the mediation process in the context of the Convention. At least conceptually, mediation has entered the Convention arena by means of the provisions on voluntary return and amicable resolution. While these provisions do provide the legal basis for its use, linking the concepts has led to some confusion as in some sectors the terms are being used synonymously.[25]

Mediation is one process through which voluntary return or amicable resolution may be achieved. However, linking the concepts has meant that to a certain degree any process through which a voluntary return or amicable resolution is achieved becomes labelled as 'mediation'. Additionally, to link these terms means that the importance and value of both mediation on the one hand, and other

[21] Interestingly, and conversely, the number and proportion of contact cases resolved by agreement decreased with 35 cases (18 per cent) in 1999, and 29 cases (13 per cent) in 2003, 2003 Study (n 4) 72–4. See also *General Principles and Guide to Good Practice on Transfrontier Contact Concerning Children* (Bristol, Family Law, 2008) [Guide on Transfrontier Contact] 6.

[22] 2003 Study (n 4) 31.

[23] ibid.

[24] 'Comments Received on the Proposal by Switzerland for a Protocol to the Hague Convention of 25 October 1980 on the Civil Aspects of International Child Abduction' Prel. Doc. No 12/2008 http://www.hcch.net/upload/wop/genaff_pd12_2008.pdf.

[25] 2006 Responses (n 1) 44–54, 264–89; Questionnaire Responses (ch 1, n 24).

processes used to reach voluntary return and amicable resolution on the other, can be somewhat diluted. The 1999 and 2003 Studies revealed that to some extent the priority placed upon seeking voluntary return appears to affect outcome. States which systematically seek voluntary return prior to the court hearing generally report a higher proportion of voluntary returns, whereas in States which pass applications quickly into the court process the obligation to seek a voluntary return can be somewhat overlooked.[26] Disputes which can be resolved informally are likely to reach conclusion quicker and with less emotional and financial cost, which is certainly in the interests of the child.[27] Therefore such processes should not be underestimated or overlooked owing to the current enthusiasm around the instigation of mediation.[28] In several states Central Authorities seek to encourage a voluntary return or an amicable resolution either before instigating court procedures or as a first step in this process. These efforts can be extremely effective.

There are also benefits inherent in the mediation process which may be absent from other processes designed to secure voluntary resolution.[29] The second definitional distinction is therefore made between 'mediation' and the Convention concepts of 'voluntary return' and 'amicable resolution', as mediation is only one specific means through which voluntary return or amicable resolution may be achieved.

C. Defining Mediation

Cross-border instruments which refer to mediation tend to avoid definition largely because in the context of the application of the instrument any mediation process would take place in the domestic system of the relevant Contracting State and therefore fall within the competence of that State. Where attempts have been made to define the process, broad definitions are generally used in order to be inclusive as mediation is often undefined, ill defined or differently defined in different States. The first and still the only significant text drafted at the international level on the specific subject of family mediation is the 1998 Council of Europe Recommendation

[26] N Lowe et al, 'A Statistical Analysis of Applications made in 2003 under the Hague Convention of 25 October 1980 on the Civil Aspects of International Child Abduction: Part II: National Reports' Prel. Doc. No 3/2008 (2007 update) http://hcch.evision.nl/upload/wop/abd_pd03ef2007.pdf [2003 Study – National Reports]. See also P Beaumont and P McEleavy, *The Hague Convention on International Child Abduction* (Oxford, Oxford University Press, 1999) [Beaumont & McEleavy] 246; S Armstrong, 'Is the Jurisdiction of England and Wales Correctly Applying the 1980 Hague Convention on the Civil Aspects of International Child Abduction?' (2002) 51 *ICLQ* 427.

[27] There is no available data on applications which were amicably resolved but did not result in return. Some of the cases which were categorised as 'withdrawn' in the two Studies may have been withdrawn because agreement was reached; however, this is generally not known and further research would be interesting.

[28] See A Bucher, 'The New Swiss Federal Act on International Child Abduction' (2008) 4 *Journal of Private International Law* 139 [Bucher 2008] 147.

[29] ch 4, III.B.

on Family Mediation.[30] No attempt was made at a formal definition in the text itself but the Explanatory Memorandum gave some guidance on the meaning of mediation and the role of mediators:

> mediation [is] a process in which a third party, who has no vested interest in the matters in dispute, facilitates discussion between the parties in order to help them to resolve their difficulties and reach agreements . . . the mediator has no authority to impose a solution on the parties but should remain both neutral and impartial. The mediator's role is to help the parties negotiate together and to reach their own joint agreements.[31]

This Recommendation though primarily addressing family mediation at a domestic level does contain some provision for international cases[32]. Additionally, in the federal and regional contexts there is some regulation of cross border mediation, which includes, but is not restricted to, family mediation. Within the United States and the European Union mediation is defined in both legislation[33] and codes of conduct for mediators.[34] The United States Uniform Mediation Act defines mediation as 'a process in which a mediator facilitates communication and negotiation between parties to assist them in reaching a voluntary agreement regarding their dispute'.[35] The European Mediation Directive defines mediation as 'a structured process . . . whereby two or more parties to a dispute attempt by themselves, on a voluntary basis, to reach an agreement on the settlement of their dispute with the assistance of a mediator'.[36] In both texts the meaning of 'mediator' ensures that these definitions are viewed broadly and inclusively. In the former a mediator is 'an individual who conducts a mediation'[37] and in the latter 'any third person who is asked to conduct a mediation in an effective, impartial and competent way, regardless of the denomination or profession of that third party'.[38] These definitions are wide enough to embrace almost all types of assisted dispute resolution, with the exception of litigation and adjudication, which is expressly excluded.[39]

[30] Recommendation No R(98)1 of the Committee of Ministers to Member States on Family Mediation (adopted by the Committee of Ministers on 21 January 1998) www.coe.int/t/e/legal_affairs/legal_co-operation/family_law_and_children%27s_rights/conferences/Rec(98)1%20E.pdf [Council of Europe Recommendation].

[31] 'Explanatory Memorandum to Recommendation No R(98)1 of the Committee of Ministers to Member States on Family Mediation' [Council of Europe Memorandum] [16].

[32] Art VIII.

[33] Uniform Mediation Act drafted by the National Conference of Commissioners on Uniform State Laws 2001 (last revised or amended in 2003) [Uniform Mediation Act]; Directive 2008/52/EC of the European Parliament and of the Council of 21 May 2008 on certain aspects of mediation in civil and commercial matters [Mediation Directive] .

[34] Model Standards of Conduct for Mediators 2005, adopted by the American Arbitration Association (8 September 2005), American Bar Association (9 August 2005), and the Association for Conflict Resolution (22 August 2005); Code of Conduct for Mediators (Brussels, July 2004) [European Code of Conduct].

[35] Uniform Mediation Act (n 33) s 2(1).

[36] Mediation Directive (n 33) Art 3(a).

[37] Uniform Mediation Act (n 33) s 2(3).

[38] Mediation Directive (n 33) Art 3(b).

[39] Uniform Mediation Act (n 33) s 2(1) comment [2]; Mediation Directive (n 33) Art 3(a).

In the absence of more precise legislative definitions some family mediators have themselves formed organisations to devise training standards and shared definitions with a view to harmonising family mediation at a cross-border level. Federal,[40] regional[41] and linguistic-based[42] organisations have provided helpful definitions. A group of family mediators meeting under the auspices of the International Social Service proposed the following:

> Family mediation is a process in which qualified and impartial third parties (mediators) assist the parties to negotiate directly or indirectly on the issues that need to be resolved and to reach considered and mutually acceptable decisions that reduce conflict and encourage co-operation for the well-being of all concerned.[43]

This definition recognises the importance of mediator qualification; what mediation aims to achieve in resolving issues; and some of the benefits of the process. That mediation aims to resolve the dispute whilst also improving relationships is very important and a section of this book is devoted to discussing the benefits inherent in the mediation process.[44] However, for the purposes of defining the discipline it is suggested that further clarification is primarily needed regarding key elements of the process, namely that mediation is voluntary and confidential and that mediated agreements are not legally binding. Clarity on these issues is necessary if mediation is to develop harmoniously across different States. Thus, while it is difficult to propose a formal definition without some discussion at the multilateral level, a working description of mediation which draws from generally agreed principles is proposed as a starting point:[45]

[40] Notable in the United States is the Model Standards of Practice for Family and Divorce Mediation, developed by the Symposium on Standards of Practice in August 2000 www.afccnet.org/pdfs/model-standards.pdf.

[41] European family mediators produced a European Charter on training for family mediation in 1992. A European Forum for Family Mediation Training and Research was formally constituted and standards for training were revised in Hamburg (January 2000) and further updated in Paris (January 2003). The European Forum defines mediation as: 'a process in which a specially trained third party is requested by the parties to help them deal with the re-ordering of their arrangements following their separation, in the context of current legislation. Family mediators seek to re-establish communication between couples to help them reach concrete decisions in relation to their post-separation parenting and financial arrangements', in L Parkinson, 'Family Mediation in Europe – divided or united?' updated paper given at: 'European Masters in Mediation' (Sion, Switzerland, March 2003) [Parkinson 2003].

[42] *Association internationale francophone des intervenants auprès des familles séparées* (AIFI) is an organisation for francophone mediators which defines mediation as: 'un processus par lequel un tiers impartial et qualifié, dûment accrédité, accompagne des couples séparés ou en voie de séparation, résidant dans deux pays différents à établir ou rétablir une communication et à trouver ensemble des accords tenant compte des besoins de chacun et particulièrement des enfants dans un esprit de coopération parentale', 'Feasibility Study on Cross-border Mediation in Family Matters – Responses to the Questionnaire' Prel. Doc. No 10/2008 www.hcch.net/upload/wop/genaff_pd10_2008.pdf [Feasibility Study Responses] 21.

[43] International Social Service Family Mediation Trainers Group (Geneva 2005) in L Parkinson, 'Cross-Border Family Mediation: Opportunities, Difficulties and Experience' (ERA Conference on Cross-Border Family Mediation, Trier, Germany, April 2007) [Parkinson 2007].

[44] ch 4, III.B.

[45] Generally agreed principles which support this working description can be found in, inter alia: Council of Europe Recommendation (n 30); Mediation Directive (n 33); Uniform Mediation Act (n 33); 2006 Responses (n 1); Questionnaire Responses (ch 1, n 24); family mediator definitions.

> Mediation is a voluntary and confidential process through which parties can reach their own agreements, which are not legally binding. Mediation is undertaken with the assistance of a trained and qualified mediator who is impartial, independent and neutral.

This working description has two strands. Firstly, it seeks to describe the essential elements of the process; and secondly, it seeks to describe the role of the mediators. It does not seek to establish one particular method or style of mediation, as there should be room for flexibility as States develop their processes.

By way of summary the following points of process should be emphasised. Mediation is voluntary and thus requires there to be an alternative option.[46] Indeed, the notion of compelling a person to negotiate is both conceptually and practically difficult. Mediation is also confidential, which has implications particularly for the interaction between the mediation process and any subsequent court process.[47] In mediation the parties are responsible for decision-making, while the mediator's role is to manage the process. Finally, agreements reached in mediation are not legally binding; however, there should be mechanisms to enable agreements to be made enforceable.[48]

With regard to mediators, firstly they must be trained and qualified as mediators.[49] In the Convention context this distinguishes mediation from negotiations led by judges, lawyers and Central Authority staff. It is recommended that such negotiations should not be termed 'mediation' and that where these professionals are additionally qualified as mediators and are in fact undertaking a mediation process, they should only do so in cases where they are not also acting in another professional capacity.[50] The role of a mediator also requires impartiality, which means that the mediator treats each party equally and does not represent either party or favour either perspective. Additionally, mediators are independent and are thus not connected in any way to either party. Finally, mediators are neutral as to outcome, which emphasises that the parties devise their own solutions and the mediator must allow them to do so.

It is hoped that this description is broad enough to encompass many different styles of mediation and to allow for continued creativity as the discipline develops; yet narrow enough to ensure clarity of understanding. Having a clear focus will allow a framework to develop against which mediation can be evaluated and assessed.

[46] ch 2, III.
[47] ch 3, III.E.
[48] ch 3, III.H
[49] ch 3, III.I.
[50] Under the Mediation Directive (n 33) mediation 'includes mediation conducted by a judge who is not responsible for any judicial proceedings concerning the dispute in question. It excludes attempts made by the court or the judge seised to settle a dispute in the course of judicial proceedings concerning the dispute in question' Art 3(a).

D. The Mediation Process

To offer further clarity regarding what mediation is it is necessary briefly to discuss two additional points. Firstly, that the mediation process requires the support of the legal system; and secondly, that the mediation process comprises two essential components: individual intake sessions and joint mediation sessions.

i. Legal Structures to Support Mediation

The success of mediation rests to a large extent on the effectiveness of the legal system which underpins it. The law plays an 'important role in encouraging the effective use of mediation and maintaining its integrity, as well as the appropriate relationship of mediation with the justice system'.[51] 'If a supporting structure of legal norms and procedures is absent, there is a real danger of imbalance or even abuse of the bargaining process'.[52] As a result it is important to ensure that the legal system which underpins Convention mediation is adequate.

In the Convention context the legal framework which supports mediation should be viewed broadly. It encompasses rules established by the provisions of the instrument itself; and rules of domestic law and procedure which govern both the application of the Convention and the mediation process. The Convention itself establishes clear rules for handling a return application which adequately support a mediation process by providing the alternative to mediation and the backdrop against which mediation takes place. It is for this reason that focus is on applications for return rather than applications for contact, where legal structures are weaker; and on Convention applications rather than child abduction more generally, where there may be an absence of supporting structures. The use of mediation to handle applications for contact or abduction falling outside the Convention is certainly to be encouraged and might be the most appropriate way to deal with these cases.[53] However, this book focuses on Convention return applications where there is a solid legal framework. It is hoped that addressing mediation in this context will assist mediation to develop as a useful tool in cross-border family disputes more generally.

Contracting States must also ensure that their domestic framework for handling Convention applications is adequate to support mediation. Mediation should never be seen as an answer to a failing court system and the development of mediation in the Convention context should not be to the detriment of improving legal processes. Rather, various features of a legal regime which support the operation of the Convention, such as the concentration of jurisdiction to a

[51] Uniform Mediation Act (n 33) [Introduction].

[52] 'Feasibility Study on Cross-Border Mediation in Family Matters' Prel. Doc. No 20/2007 www.hcch.net/upload/wop/genaff_pd20e2007.pdf [2007 Feasibility Study] 23; W Duncan, 'Transfrontier Access/Contact General Principles and Good Practice' Prel. Doc. No 4/2006 http://hcch.e-vision.nl/upload/wop/abd_pd04e2006.pdf [Duncan 2006] 13.

[53] In this regard the Hague Conference is involved in some very important initiatives, highlighted at ch 1, n 18. See also ch 4, III.C.

limited number of courts or judges, and continued training for Convention practitioners,[54] will equally support the operation of the mediation process.

A State's procedure for handling a Convention application must be adequate such that the introduction of a mediation process would not cause undue delay or detract from the application of the instrument. There must be adequate pathways into and out of mediation and there must be good interaction between the mediation process and the other aspects of the procedure; as well as good interaction between the different professionals involved in handling the application. In this regard, one of the key objectives underlying the reunite scheme was 'to develop a mediation structure that would fit in practically with the procedural structure of an English Hague Convention case'.[55] It was recognised that 'it was of paramount importance that the UK's reputation as an enthusiastic and reliable upholder of the Hague Convention should not be undermined'.[56] Without taking away from the achievement of reunite, it is without doubt that one of the reasons for the success of this project is that it operated squarely within, and was supported by, a well-functioning procedure for handling Convention cases. States wishing to develop Convention mediation should ensure that their domestic procedure for handling a Convention application is adequate to support a mediation process.

Equally there must be adequate structures to regulate the mediation process including the training and qualification of mediators. Certainly the development of Convention mediation is likely to be influenced by the perception, and status, of domestic family mediation in the particular State. The extent to which States have a sufficient regulatory framework to support Convention mediation differs.[57] Family mediation has 'been used for a long time in traditional societies for the resolution of disputes within communities and kinship systems'.[58] States in the Far East, notably China and Japan,[59] have a long history of mediation as do certain Islamic traditions[60] and certain cultures in Africa and the Caribbean.[61] Interestingly, the majority of these States remain outside the Convention regime.[62]

In many other States, particularly in Central and Eastern Europe, which have largely embraced the Convention, and also former Soviet States, family mediation

[54] Conclusions of experts' meetings www.hcch.net/index_en.php?act=text.display&tid= 21#network.

[55] reunite, 'Mediation in International Parental Child Abduction: The reunite Mediation Pilot Scheme' (October 2006) www.reunite.org/edit/files/Mediation%20Report.pdf [reunite Report] 6.

[56] ibid 7.

[57] In some States family mediation is 'still very recent and enjoys neither the development nor diffusion necessary to think about a systematization of the procedure for cases so specific' as child abduction, Feasibility Study Responses (n 42) 6, response of Argentina.

[58] Council of Europe Memorandum (n 31) [16].

[59] See S Minamikata, 'Resolution of Disputes over Parental Rights and Duties in a Marital Dissolution Case in Japan: A Non-litigious Approach in *Chotei* (Family Court Mediation)' [2005-06] 39 *Family Law Quarterly* 489 [Minamikata 2006]; K Funken, 'Comparative Dispute Management: Court-connected Mediation in Japan and Germany' (2002) 3 *German Law Journal.*

[60] M Keshavjee, 'Family Mediation in the Shia Imami Ismaili Muslim Community – Institutional Structures, Training and Practice' (2009 Strasbourg Conference) (n 3).

[61] A Fiadjoe, 'Family Mediation in the Caribbean' (2009 Strasbourg Conference) (n 3).

[62] All States entitled to ratify the Convention have done so with the exception of Japan and Egypt both of which have a strong tradition of mediation. See also ch 1, n 18.

remains relatively unknown.[63] One commentator notes that 'mediation assumes a certain level of development of civil society and a certain level of personal autonomy and personal freedom and, accordingly, personal responsibility.'[64] She further notes that in some of these States 'these are characteristics that still need to be developed' and that '[c]ultural barriers . . . may significantly complicate using family mediation for resolution of cross-border disputes'.[65] However, there is some evidence of movement towards a greater use of family mediation in some of these States,[66] and the Mediation Directive is likely to act as a catalyst in those States which are members of the European Union.

A third category of States includes the Americas, Western Europe, Australia and New Zealand. In these traditionally litigious cultures family dispute resolution rested almost solely within the realm of the courts until the late 1970s when the modern family mediation movement arrived on a wave of enthusiasm. It was described as a 'dream' and compared with the 'nightmare of justice',[67] and was heralded as a 'panacea for dealing with the rapidly increasing divorce rate and enormous backlogs in the courts'.[68] It is perhaps not surprising that it is predominantly these States which are pressing forward with Convention mediation.

In seeking to advance mediation in the Convention context it is necessary to be cognisant of the fact that Contracting States are at very different stages in terms of the development or institutionalisation of domestic family mediation. There are legal differences in terms of the regulation of mediation, notably the training of mediators; and there are cultural differences and perceptions of mediation.[69] Against this backdrop it is likely that Convention mediation will continue to develop on a piecemeal basis. Indeed, some States may not be in a position to offer mediation in Convention cases, particularly those States which have very little experience of mediation in the domestic context.

[63] 2006 Responses (n 1) 264–89.

[64] O Khazova, 'Prospects of International Family Mediation in Russia' (2009 Strasbourg Conference) (n 3).

[65] ibid.

[66] ibid, and J Arsić, 'Family Mediation Concerning Couples of Different Ethnic Origin in the Region of the Former Yugoslavia' (2009 Strasbourg Conference) (n 3). See also 2006 Responses (n 1) 52, 269 and 281 where Cyprus, Lithuania and Romania refer to proposed family mediation legislation.

[67] L Dumoulin, 'La médiation familiale est-elle « une utopie qui réussit » ? D'une technique de résolution des conflits a un projet social et politique' paper presented in October 2003, and cited in D Macfarlane, 'Family Mediation in France' (2004) 10 *Journal of Family Studies* 97 [Macfarlane 2004].

[68] Macfarlane 2004 (n 67).

[69] Culture is a complex phenomenon which may impact upon a person's ability to negotiate, and his perception of the value of mediation. There may be cases where as a result a mediator decides that mediation is not appropriate, or that additional safeguards are required. The implications of culture on mediation are important. For discussion see: H Abramson, 'Selecting Mediators and Representing Clients in Cross-Cultural Disputes' (2006) 7.2 *Cardozo Journal Conflict Resolution* 253; J Gold, 'ADR Through a Cultural Lens: How Cultural Values Shape our Disputing Processes' (2005) *Journal of Dispute Resolution* 289; M Roberts, 'International Family Mediation and Recommendation No R(98)1: A Chronicle of Expansion Foretold' (2008) *International Family Law* 217; S Shah-Kazemi, 'Cross-Cultural Mediation: A Critical View of the Dynamics of Culture in Family Disputes' (2000) 14 *International Journal of Law Policy and the Family* 326; J Zawid, 'Practical and Ethical Implications of Mediating International Child Abduction Cases: A New Frontier for Mediators' (2008) 40 *University of Miami Inter-American Law Review* 1 [Zawid 2008].

ii. Aspects of the Mediation Process

The mediation process comprises two important steps: firstly the individual intake sessions and secondly the joint mediation sessions. An individual intake session is an essential first step in the mediation process. The purpose of this session is threefold: for the mediator to provide information to the party about the mediation process and the alternate court process; for the party to provide information to the mediator about the issues of the dispute; and for the mediator to screen for domestic violence and child safety concerns.[70] Each of these elements is vital to the integrity of the mediation process. Parties need information about their options so they can make an informed decision about whether they wish to proceed and the mediator needs information about the subject matter of the dispute in order to make a decision as to whether the case is suitable for mediation.[71] Parties should have the opportunity to raise issues about their situation initially in confidence without the other party being present. Where child protection concerns are raised mediation will generally not be appropriate and allegations will require investigation.[72] Where domestic violence issues are raised the mediator and the party need to decide whether mediation can progress and if so what safeguards need to be established.[73] Intake sessions thus ensure mediation is voluntary – on the part of each party and the mediator; suitable – given the subject matter; and safe.

If both parties and the mediator agree the case can proceed to a joint mediation session. Joint sessions should preferably take place with both parties together meeting face-to-face.[74] However, this is not always possible and parties can mediate in the same location but in separate rooms (caucusing or shuttle mediation);[75] or by distance telecommunications such as the Internet, telephone or video-conferencing facilities, if the parties are in different States.[76] The reference to 'joint' session does not therefore imply that the parties must be in the same physical location but rather that they are both involved in the negotiations, unlike individual intake sessions.

It is suggested that to promote harmonious development of Convention mediation a checklist of important issues to cover in intake sessions should be considered at the multilateral level. Additional questions could then be added on

[70] Mediation providers must operate within a child protection and a domestic violence policy.

[71] eg if parties are seeking to alter legal rights or obligations this would fall outside the scope of mediation.

[72] In the reunite scheme '[i]t was agreed that if during mediation a child protection issue arose, the mediation would cease and the appropriate child protection agencies would be contacted', reunite Report (n 55) 11.

[73] See ch 4, II.C.

[74] ch 3, III.G.

[75] Caucusing and shuttle mediation essentially involve the mediator meeting separately with each party and moving between them, which can be particularly appropriate where domestic violence has been raised.

[76] ch 3, III.G.

a State-by-State basis to take account of specific procedural issues.[77] Additionally, some States have developed an 'Agreement to Mediate' which parties are required to sign prior to commencing joint mediation.[78] Such Agreements help to establish appropriate expectations and provide a formal backdrop for negotiations; they can also clearly stipulate various key rules such as those relating to confidentiality. This also might be a useful document to draft at the multilateral level with the option to add specific procedural elements on a State-by-State basis as required.

III. Place in the Procedure

A. Introduction

The first part of this chapter sought to promote movement towards a greater use of Convention mediation by offering definitional clarity. This second part seeks to further add clarity and enhance understanding by providing an outline of the place of mediation in the procedure for handling a Convention application. Indeed it was noted by the 2006 Special Commission that the 'integration [of mediation] within the framework of the Convention should be carefully considered'.[79] It is suggested that mediation should be viewed generally as one aspect of the broader procedure for handling the Convention application, and specifically as an alternative to the court hearing.[80]

At the outset of this discussion it is necessary to emphasise that the enduring appeal of the Convention, which continues to attract new States, in part rests on the fact that it is not prescriptive. Contracting States have the freedom to implement and apply the instrument within the parameters of their current system, provided they use the 'most expeditious procedures available'.[81] Therefore it would be contrary to the spirit of the instrument and potentially damaging in relations between States if the place of mediation or the methodology for mediation was too rigidly dictated. Rather this part of the chapter seeks to offer a general outline of how a mediation process can fit within the Convention procedure

[77] reunite has constructed such a checklist, on file with author. The organisation Global Justice Initiative in the United States has also developed intake forms which screen for domestic violence, information from Julia Alanen; Questionnaire Responses (ch 1, n 24) Judge Carl.

[78] For an example: BAFM Agreement to Mediate www.bafmmediation.de/International/english/agreement-to-mediate/ [BAFM Agreement to Mediate].

[79] 'Report on the Fifth Meeting of the Special Commission to Review the Operation of the Hague Convention of 25 October 1980 on the Civil Aspects of International Child Abduction and the Practical Implementation of the Hague Convention of 19 October 1996 on Jurisdiction, Applicable Law, Recognition, Enforcement and Co-Operation in respect of Parental Responsibility and Measures for the Protection of Children' (October–November 2006) Prel. Doc. No 19/2007 http://hcch.e-vision.nl/upload/wop/genaff_pd19e2007.pdf [2006 Report] [64].

[80] Details of how the mediation process can operate within the constraints of the Convention are the subject matter of chapter three.

[81] Art 2.

notwithstanding the diversity of implementation and application across the range of Contracting States.

B. The Place of Convention Mediation

Viewing mediation as one aspect of the broader procedure for handling a Convention application has several advantages. Firstly, it ensures that mediation is a means of applying the instrument not a method through which the Convention can be avoided. Secondly, certain issues of importance can be dealt with in the context of the broader procedure rather than as an element of the mediation process itself.[82] Thirdly, the mediation process can benefit from any advantageous regime established for Convention applications. Fourthly, situating mediation within the broader procedure means that it sits squarely within the legal framework of the Convention.

More specifically, mediation as a formal method of dispute resolution should be viewed as an alternative to the court hearing phase. This, however, does not mean that the former is a substitute for the latter; rather, the mediation process relies upon the alternate court hearing for a number of reasons. Firstly, the alternative court process ensures that mediation can be voluntary. Secondly, it provides the backdrop for negotiation, defining its scope. Thirdly, where parties cannot reach agreement in mediation the court process subsists as the means to resolve the dispute.

i. Provision of Information

Offering mediation as an alternative to the court hearing means that parties need information about the two processes in order to make an informed decision as to which route to take. Thought must be given to how information is provided. In Switzerland a particular body is mandated to provide information to parties in a Convention dispute.[83] A Central Authority in another State noted that it was 'looking at what information may assist parties and [in] what format that information is to be provided'.[84] In the reunite scheme '[i]t was recognised that the manner in which both parents were introduced to the scheme was critical to its prospects of success.'[85] It is suggested that States must make information available at the outset of the proceedings. Such information should be offered via the Internet so that it is accessible regardless of where parties are located, and in hard copy. All Convention practitioners, including Central Authorities, non-governmental organisations,

[82] One such issue is how to hear the child, which is discussed fully in chapter five.

[83] Arrêté fédéral portant mise en œuvre des conventions sur l'enlèvement international d'enfants et portant approbation et mise en œuvre des Conventions de La Haye sur la protection des enfants et des adultes du 21 décembre 2007, Feuille Fédérale No 1 (2008) 33–40 RS 211.222.32 www.admin.ch/ch/f/ff/2008/33.pdf [Swiss legislation] Art 3(2).

[84] Questionnaire Responses (ch 1, n 24) New Zealand Central Authority.

[85] reunite Report (n 55) 8.

lawyers and the courts, should be able to provide the relevant information to ensure that parties have access to the mediation process regardless of which body they contact first. Particular attention should be given to ensuring that the body which acts as the point of first contact in Convention applications has adequate information. Mediation must not cause undue delay[86] and therefore parties need to be aware of their options upfront. At an initial intake meeting with a mediator or an initial meeting with a lawyer, the parties can also be reminded of their options before committing to either process.

ii. Instigating Mediation

As an alternative to the court hearing the option to mediate does not replace informal negotiations to seek voluntary resolution, but rather follows if these negotiations fail. Failure of the latter does not imply that the former will not succeed; just as failure of informal negotiations does not preclude a subsequent court order being made by consent. In some States informal negotiations are a distinct first step in the procedure while in others seeking voluntary resolution is primarily left to the lawyers once the court process is underway. As mediation is a flexible process it can fit within a State's current procedure. Therefore where informal negotiations proceed as a distinct first step, perhaps between the abductor and the Central Authority, mediation can follow if the abductor does not agree to return the child. Alternatively, where the case would normally go straight into the legal system and informal negotiations to seek voluntary resolution are incorporated as a first step in the court process, the same could happen in mediation. Mediators can verify during the intake session whether, for example, the abducting parent would be willing to return the child voluntarily without the need to progress to a joint mediation session.[87]

Mediation is an alternative to the court hearing on the issue of the application. As such, it is not a replacement for a preliminary ruling. In some States it is normal practice to have a preliminary ruling at which safeguards might be put in place, such as the confiscation of passports to prevent further removal. Timelines also might be set to ensure expeditious action.[88] Such a ruling can be useful prior to instigating a mediation process as a court may be asked to 'fix a deadline for an agreement to be reached in order to ensure that mediation [is] quick and efficient and to ensure that parents [are] moving towards a workable solution'.[89] In this regard mediation under the reunite scheme:

> was only embarked upon once an application for a return had been issued and had been heard on an initial hearing by the court. The court would place safeguards to ensure the child was not moved to another country or place of hiding.[90]

[86] See ch 3, III.C.

[87] Of the 80 referrals made to reunite three resulted in voluntary return prior to mediation, reunite Report (n 55) 12.

[88] ibid 7.

[89] 2006 Report (n 79) [63].

[90] reunite Report (n 55) 7.

In other States Convention applications proceed by way of a single hearing on the issues. In Germany the court first hears the case but can refer the parties to mediation before the decision is handed down.[91] Following from the court hearing means that safeguards can be put in place if necessary, similar to a preliminary ruling. However, it is an unusual practice to mediate after a contested battle in court. As one commentator has put it, 'mediation should be to family matters as diplomacy is to war: a first step and not a last chance solution when everything else has failed and it is really too late'.[92] Indeed, one of the perceived benefits of mediation is the avoidance of the adversarial court process and the increased animosity that may result from this.[93] Therefore conducting a full hearing prior to mediation is not recommended, rather mediation should be offered as an alternative to the court hearing.

iii. Mediation and the Court Hearing are not Equivalent

While it is suggested that mediation should be viewed as an alternative to the court hearing because mediation and the court process are both formal mechanisms through which the application can be resolved, mediation and the court process are not equivalents. Encouraging a greater use of mediation should not usurp the important and necessary role of the courts in Convention cases.

Some parties will choose to pursue their case in court notwithstanding the option to mediate. In a limited number of States there is some degree of compulsion regarding domestic family mediation, usually to attend an intake session prior to pursuing an application in court.[94] In Switzerland, Convention legislation obliges the court to 'initiate' 'mediation procedures' if the Central Authority, which has discretion to initiate such procedures, has not already done so.[95] While there may be benefits in compelling parties to attend an intake session in domestic family law cases, in child abduction cases there is broad agreement 'that mediation must be voluntary' and 'recourse to mediation should not be automatic'.[96] Indeed, insisting that parties must attend an intake session could cause delay. The very existence of the Convention provides a legal remedy and mediation must be offered as a voluntary alternative to the Convention court hearing, not a means of usurping the instrument or denying a party his legal right to respectively bring and defend a Convention application in court.

[91] Questionnaire Responses (ch 1, n 24) Judge Carl.

[92] D Ganancia, ' La médiation familiale internationale: une solution d'avenir aux conflits familiaux transfrontaliers ?' in H Fulchiron (ed), *Les enlèvements d'enfants à travers les frontière* (Brussels, Bruylant, 2004) [Author's translation].

[93] Convention mediation which took place in Germany between a German mother and an American father following protracted court proceedings led the parents to state that they wished mediation had occurred earlier. They felt that court proceedings had intensified the situation and mediation 'would be the only realistic way in such a case', C Paul and J Walker, 'Family Mediation in International Child Custody Conflicts: The Role of the Consulting Attorneys' (2008) *American Journal of Family Law* 42, 45.

[94] 2007 Feasibility Study (n 52) 5–6.

[95] Swiss legislation (n 83) 'The court *shall initiate* conciliation or mediation procedures' Art 8(1); 'The central authority *may initiate* a conciliation or mediation procedure' [emphasis added] Art 4(1).

[96] 2006 Report (n 79) [64].

Other cases will not be suitable for mediation and will rely on the courts for resolution.[97] Additionally, where parties opt to mediate their dispute but do not reach agreement on the primary issue of the child's residence, the case will fall to be resolved by the courts. Conversely, where parties use the court process, the outcome, though subject to appeal which may involve an option to mediate,[98] is final and the parties should not be allowed to re-examine the issues in mediation. To allow mediation to have such a role undermines the authority of the courts and could seriously hinder the swift enforcement of return orders.

A distinction should be drawn between, on the one hand, the use of mediation as a means of assisting in the effective enforcement of an order, which can be beneficial and is placed on a statutory footing in some States;[99] and on the other hand, the use of mediation to re-examine the issues, which should not be permitted. In Switzerland each canton is required to designate a single authority responsible for enforcing decisions and this authority 'shall . . . endeavour to obtain the voluntary execution of the decision'.[100] This provision refers to the former issue of seeking to secure voluntary enforcement of an order. However, Professor Bucher states that:

> [w]hile this is not contained in the rule itself, it is implied that the authority in charge may also open a debate on the question of whether the parents would be willing to agree on a settlement in which the return order would not be enforced.[101]

It is submitted that this should not be the accepted interpretation of this provision as it would allow mediation to usurp a court order. Indeed a Contracting State has drawn attention to two cases where the foreign Central Authority sought to initiate a mediation process suggesting that the left-behind parent consider allowing the children to stay, notwithstanding that the court had already ordered return.[102] This State 'suggested that this is an inappropriate use of the mediation process, and that once a court issues an order for return, the central authorities must act to ensure the immediate return of the children'.[103] It is submitted that this is the correct view and mediation should not be used as a means to circumvent an order.

On the other hand, the Swiss legislation allows a court to make a new order where prior to enforcement the circumstances 'change in a significant manner'.[104]

[97] eg where parties are simply not willing to negotiate or make decisions for themselves. See also ch 2, II. D. ii.

[98] The use of mediation during the appeals process has been found to be 'successful in a number of cases', Questionnaire Responses (ch 1, n 24) Judge Carl. See also *Al-Khatib v Masry* [2004] EWCA 1353 [17].

[99] eg in Sweden 'Act on Recognition and Enforcement of Foreign Decisions concerning Custody, etc., and on the Return of Children (1989:14)' [Swedish legislation] [ss 13–21]; A Schulz, 'Enforcement of Orders made under the 1980 Convention – Towards Principles of Good Practice' Prel. Doc. No 7/2006 http://hcch.e-vision.nl/upload/wop/abd_pd07e2006.pdf [Enforcement Reports].

[100] Swiss legislation (n 83) Art 12. The original French reads: 'L'autorité tient compte de l'intérêt de l'enfant et s'efforce d'obtenir l'exécution volontaire de la décision'.

[101] Bucher 2008 (n 28) 153.

[102] 2006 Responses (n 1) 286 Israel.

[103] ibid.

[104] Art 13.

With regard to this latter provision Professor Bucher states that the 'focus will be solely on circumstances . . . that would comply with the requirements and the limited scope of possible objections under the Hague Convention'.[105] Additionally, 'the change of circumstances should be significant. There will be no possibility to relitigate the return order unless the situation has, in its relevant parts, changed dramatically'.[106] This strict interpretation of the latter provision is in line with the jurisprudence of the European Court of Human Rights, which has also taken a very narrow approach to the circumstances in which a court might re-examine the issues.[107] Thus mediation can be useful at the enforcement stage but should not be used to avoid a return order. In rare cases where return is no longer appropriate it should be left to the courts to make a new order.

Similarly, where parties reach agreement in mediation, thus resolving the Convention application and this agreement becomes enforceable,[108] parties should not be permitted to renege on the agreement and bring another application under the Convention. For mediation to be a useful alternative to a court order parties need assurance that if they reach agreement and formalise this agreement they can act in reliance upon its terms. This would need to be made known to parties at the outset so that they are fully aware of the consequences of formalising a mediated agreement.

iv. The Focus of Mediation

It is a well-established principle that parties in mediation do not negotiate in a vacuum, rather they 'bargain in the shadow of the law'.[109] In other words, 'the outcome that the law will impose if no agreement is reached gives each party certain bargaining chips',[110] and the extent to which a negotiated agreement is acceptable tends to depend upon the extent to which it improves upon a party's 'best alternative to a negotiated agreement',[111] usually a court-ordered solution. Although mediation stands outside the court case it is recognised that 'private ordering between the parties themselves is influenced by knowledge of what the court would be likely to order, if the dispute is taken to court'.[112]

[105] Bucher 2008 (n 28) 154.

[106] ibid.

[107] The court has stated that 'a change in the relevant facts may exceptionally justify the non-enforcement of a final return order' provided that the change 'was not brought about by the States' failure to take all measures that could reasonably be expected to facilitate execution of the order', *Sylvester v Austria* [2003] ECtHR nos 36812/97 and 40104/98 [63]. See also observations of the New Zealand Court of Appeal in *Butler v Craig* [2008] NZCA 198, discussed in P Beaumont, 'The Jurisprudence of the European Court of Human Rights and the European Court of Justice on the Hague Convention on International Child Abduction' in *Recueil des cours: volume 335 (2008)* (Leiden, Martinus Nijhoff Publishers, 2009) 81–4.

[108] ch 3, III.H.

[109] R Mnookin and L Kornhauser, 'Bargaining in the Shadow of the Law: The Case of Divorce' (1979) 88 *Yale Law Journal* 950, 968.

[110] ibid.

[111] R Fisher; W Ury and B Patton, *Getting to Yes – Negotiating an agreement without giving in*, 2nd edn (London Random House, 1991).

[112] Parkinson 2003 (n 41).

The Convention essentially envisages a two-step process: the Convention case which is primarily an issue of forum; and the subsequent case dealing with the merits of the dispute. Convention mediation must take place against the backdrop of both these cases viewed together. To do otherwise jeopardises the integrity of the mediation process. If mediation merely takes place against the backdrop of the return mechanism, the left-behind parent generally has a dominant bargaining position and there is therefore very little incentive for him to enter into mediation. Equally, it is unusual to conduct mediation purely in the light of a wrongful act that requires by law the return of the child.

The scope of Convention mediation is therefore broader than the Convention court hearing, but in combining the two steps into one it is also narrower than the subsequent domestic litigation on the merits. The primary focus of Convention mediation must be the child's place of residence and other issues can be negotiated only insofar as they impact upon this primary focus. Certain additional issues which go beyond the matter of the child's residence are not appropriate for discussion in Convention mediation, notwithstanding that they might have been raised in any subsequent court hearing on the merits. Challenges raised by the scope of Convention mediation are discussed in detail in chapter three.[113] For present purposes it is necessary to state that parties must be adequately informed at the outset of proceedings that the scope of mediation and the court hearing is different.

It has been noted in response to the Questionnaire that responsibility for passing on information regarding the legal regime of the Convention generally rests with lawyers.[114] In some States lawyers may 'not have any specialised knowledge of Hague Convention proceedings' and may thus advise parties 'incompletely or even incorrectly, causing those parties to have the often unrealistic expectation that they can win the case, even if their situation has no prospect of success.'[115] On the other hand, it has also been stressed that giving information on the likely outcome can reduce the chances of parties making concessions or deciding that they wish to mediate.[116] Additionally, an experienced Convention judge has noted that:

> making an unqualified and absolute declaration that . . . the applying party's return application will definitely be approved under all circumstances is a factor that can cause the applying party to reject any attempts to come to an arrangement that is mutually acceptable, at any rate if, as a judge, one does not provide any other advice.[117]

This judge described how his practice involves stating 'cautiously but clearly if the parent wishing the child's return had good prospects of success'. However, additionally he:

[113] Ch 3, III.B.
[114] (ch 1, n 24) New Zealand Central Authority; Sweden.
[115] ibid, Judge Carl.
[116] ibid, Judge Olland.
[117] ibid, Judge Carl.

> always linked this advice with the further advice that even when a party's prospects of success are relatively or completely clear, it can be very useful to carry out a mediation process in order to save the parties further expensive and nerve-wracking proceedings following the return of the child.[118]

Certainly, it is not possible or appropriate to second-guess either the Convention court decision in the specific case, or the outcome of subsequent litigation on the merits. To make an informed choice as to which process they wish to use, parties merely require an understanding of the fact that the scope of Convention mediation and the Convention court process is different.[119] It should be ensured that parties 'participate in mediation with full knowledge of the options open to them following the final decision of the court under the . . . Convention'.[120] Additionally, that parties are:

> provided with sufficient background information on the workings of the . . . Convention and realistic prospects of the practicalities and / or court outcomes to enable them to make reasonable compromises within the mediation.[121]

IV. Conclusion

This chapter sought to provide some response to the core question 'what is Convention mediation?' It highlighted that mediation is a distinct formal dispute resolution process undertaken by trained professionals and is thus to be distinguished from both informal processes to seek voluntary resolution, and negotiations led by judges or lawyers in Convention cases. It proposed a working description of this developing field with a view to clarifying the important concepts, which are discussed in more depth in subsequent chapters. It also described the two stages of the mediation process, the intake session and the joint session, and the need for mediation to be adequately supported by appropriate legal structures.

The final part of the chapter offered an outline of the place of mediation in the Convention procedure. In this respect mediation is here viewed generally as one aspect of the broader procedure for handling the Convention application. As such it must operate within the Convention regime and the details of this are discussed in chapter three. Specifically mediation does not replace existing informal mechanisms to seek a voluntary return or an amicable resolution, but is rather viewed as a voluntary alternative to the court hearing. It is not equivalent to the court hearing as where mediation fails to lead to an agreement the parties will be required to

118 ibid.

119 '[P]arents understood the range of options open to them but only because we (the mediators) explained the options and gave the parent an opportunity to ask questions as well as, where necessary, speak with their lawyer during the mediation process' reunite Report (n 55) 47.

120 Three out of four mediators replied 'yes', ibid 46.

121 In the reunite pilot project four out of six mediators when asked whether the parties had had sufficient background information replied 'yes', ibid 46.

pursue a resolution in court, whereas following a court hearing the parties should not be able to mediate subsequently to try to find a more favourable solution. Additionally, mediation puts the decision-making power into the hands of the parties and can therefore operate against not only the backdrop of the Convention court hearing, but also the subsequent domestic litigation on the issue of the child's future place of residence.

3

How Can a Mediation Process Fit Within the Constraints of the Convention?

I. Introduction

The previous chapter sought to clarify what Convention mediation is. The present chapter builds upon this foundation by responding to some of the specific challenges raised by mediating in the Convention context and answering the all important 'how' question. How can a mediation process fit within the constraints of the Convention? The movement towards the use of Convention mediation is being driven both by family mediation experts and Convention experts and the contribution of both these groups is essential to move the discipline forward. However, throughout the term 'Convention mediation' is deliberately used to express the idea that Convention mediation should be viewed as a distinct discipline which is significantly different from more general family mediation, and substantively different from the Convention court case.[1]

The present chapter is divided into two parts. The first explains why Convention mediation should be established as a specialism. The second highlights how specific challenges raised by mediating in the Convention context can be addressed within a specialised system. It is considered important at this early stage of the development of Convention mediation to discuss the breadth of relevant issues rather than focus on a few issues in more detail. Therefore the issues are not addressed comprehensively but further references are given where appropriate. It is expected that these issues will form part of the Guide to Good Practice and may also be further defined within any future Protocol to the Convention.

II. Convention Mediation as a Specialism

A. Introduction

There are several legal, procedural and practical aspects of the Convention regime which require Convention mediation to operate in a specific and somewhat unusual

[1] The implications of which are discussed in chapter four.

way when compared with other family mediation.[2] As a result 'it is necessary to introduce a different mediation practice to that of "normal" family mediation'.[3] The notion of establishing Convention mediation as a specialism has certain parallels with recognised good practice in the Convention court process and it is surely astute to draw from the valuable experience accrued in the last 25 years of the Convention's operation.[4] Certain issues have consistently been raised as beneficial including the concentration of jurisdiction[5] and the need for those operating the Convention to receive additional specific training.[6] The primary reason why concentrating jurisdiction to a limited group of well-trained practitioners adds value is precisely because the Convention court hearing differs from a usual family hearing. These differences similarly distinguish Convention mediation from general family mediation. Establishing a special system for Convention mediation also means that specific challenges raised by mediating within the constraints of the instrument can be addressed, without prejudice to differences within domestic mediation systems, which might otherwise impede development.

B. Approaches to Convention Mediation

The majority of States and organisations which have responded to questionnaires on the subject have highlighted that there is currently no specialised system for mediation in Convention cases but parties can be referred into the domestic

[2] See C Paul, 'Mediation in German-United States Cases: A Chance for the Children and Challenge for the Mediators' (7th European Conference on Family Law on International Family Mediation, Strasbourg, France, March 2009) www.coe.int/t/e/legal_affairs/legal_cooperation/family_law_and_children's_rights/Conferences/7th%20European%20Conference%20on%20Family%20Law%20on%20international%20family%20mediation.asp [2009 Strasbourg Conference] [Paul 2009].

[3] 83 per cent of mediators agreed with this statement, reunite, 'Mediation in International Parental Child Abduction: The reunite Mediation Pilot Scheme' (October 2006) www.reunite.org/edit/files/Mediation%20Report.pdf [reunite Report] 52. 'Mediation in international cases of parental child abduction is increasingly recognised as a specialism', L Parkinson, 'Developing International Family Mediation and Harmonising Standards' (2009 Strasbourg Conference) (n 2) [Parkinson 2009].

[4] Conclusions and Recommendations of the five Special Commission meetings: www.hcch.net/index_en.php?act=text.display&tid=21#sc [Conclusions of the Special Commissions]; Guide to Good Practice: *Part II on Implementing Measures* (Bristol, Family Law, 2003) [Guide on Implementing Measures] 29.

[5] Austria, China (Hong Kong Special Administrative Region), Cyprus, Germany, Finland, France, Ireland, Israel, Malta, Portugal, Romania, Sweden, Switzerland and jurisdictions of the United Kingdom have concentrated jurisdiction in Convention cases, 'Collated Responses to the Questionnaire concerning the Practical Operation of the Hague Convention of 25 October 1980 on the Civil Aspects of International Child Abduction' Prel. Doc. No 2/2006 http://hcch.e-vision.nl/upload/wop/abd_pd02efs2006.pdf [2006 Responses] 62–71; Arrêté fédéral portant mise en œuvre des conventions sur l'enlèvement international d'enfants et portant approbation et mise en œuvre des Conventions de La Haye sur la protection des enfants et des adultes du 21 décembre 2007, Feuille Fédérale No 1 (2008) 33–40 RS 211.222.32 www.admin.ch/ch/f/ff/2008/33.pdf [Swiss legislation] Art 7.

[6] See the judicial seminars section on the Hague Conference website www.hcch.net/index_en.php?act=text.display&tid=21.

mediation system.[7] However, there have been a limited number of important initiatives establishing specialist schemes for mediating Convention cases.

These specialist schemes are diverse and essentially three broad models can be identified. Firstly, in some States Convention mediation operates as a process within the State of refuge, designed by that State and generally using mediators trained in that State. For example, the work of reunite in England and Wales;[8] the work of *Mission d'aide à la médiation internationale pour les familles* (MAMIF) in France;[9] and the system in Brazil.[10] Secondly, there is the bi-national co-mediation model where the scheme itself is constructed and operated across both States and usually uses one mediator trained in each State, or connected to each State. Examples include projects between France and Germany;[11] and Germany and Poland.[12] Bilateral projects are also being considered for applications arising between Germany and the United States;[13] Mexico and the United States;[14] and Australia and New Zealand.[15] A slight variation on this approach which has been suggested is that a mediation scheme is established on a bilateral basis but the mediation takes place in the State of refuge using mediators from the State of habitual residence.[16] Thirdly, there is the 'mediation-based approach' where all relevant professionals are expected to view the application against the backdrop of mediation and to consider how mediation might assist the parties. The International Social Service has provided training on this approach in cross-border cases concerning children, including child abduction cases.[17] This concept appears to underlie the Swiss legislation although according to the International Social Service actually undertaking mediation though 'possible and often also

[7] 2006 Responses (n 5) 264–89, Austria, China (Hong Kong Special Administrative Region), Iceland, Ireland, Israel, The Netherlands, Poland and Sweden. Also in Quebec, Canada, Questionnaire Responses (ch 1, n 24) Lorraine Filion.

[8] reunite Report (n 3).

[9] MAMIF was created in 2001 within the French Ministry of Justice and mediated in cases involving a non-European Community Member State. The organisation is no longer operational.

[10] 'Feasibility Study on Cross-border Mediation in Family Matters – Responses to the Questionnaire' Prel. Doc. No 10/2008 www.hcch.net/upload/wop/genaff_pd10_2008.pdf [Feasibility Study Responses] 10 Brazil; see also J Zawid, 'Practical and Ethical Implications of Mediating International Child Abduction Cases: A New Frontier for Mediators' (2008) 40 *University of Miami Inter-American Law Review* 1 [Zawid 2008] 13–14.

[11] This was the first mediatory scheme established between two Convention States. Initially set up in 1999 cases were 'mediated' by Parliamentarians. In 2003 professional mediators from the two States took over the cases and this scheme ran until March 2006, S Vigers, 'Note on the Development of Mediation, Conciliation and Similar Means to Facilitate Agreed Solutions in Transfrontier Family Disputes Concerning Children especially in the context of the Hague Convention of 1980' Prel. Doc. No 5/2006 http://hcch.e-vision.nl/upload/wop/abd_pd05e2006.pdf [Note on the Development of Mediation].

[12] Questionnaire Responses (ch 1, n 24) German Central Authority; Judge Carl; BAFM.

[13] Questionnaire Responses (ch 1, n 24); 2006 Responses (n 5) 277–78 United States.

[14] Information from Julia Alanen, Doug Frenkel and Jennifer Zawid.

[15] Australia and New Zealand are considering a bilateral mediation scheme which is being discussed by the respective Central Authorities and the leading judiciary in the two States, information from Justice Bennett and Lord Justice Thorpe.

[16] Information from Justice Bennett.

[17] Feasibility Study Responses (n 10) 32 ISS.

desirable' is not required,[18] whereas the Swiss authorities are obliged to initiate mediation.[19] In this sense actual practice in Switzerland is more akin to the first approach above.

It is submitted that the mediation-based approach is not the best model for Convention cases. Mediation in these cases should be viewed as a process which can be used to seek to secure a resolution in support of the operation of the Convention. Mediation should be viewed as one aspect of the general procedure for handling a Convention application rather than the backdrop against which the application should be handled. Parties have a right to pursue a legal remedy in court and mediation is a voluntary alternative. Additionally, some cases will not be suitable for mediation and require resolution in court. Thus Convention practitioners should not be required to view applications against the backdrop of mediation. Rather they should view applications against the backdrop of the Convention.

Although mediation remains in its infancy, strong opinions have already developed with regard to the relative appeal of the first and second approaches described above. It is suggested that the ethos behind the bi-national co-mediation approach of using a mediator from each State is flawed and that this model can be unduly onerous. There appear to be two primary justifications for offering this approach. Firstly, so that the parties perceive the process to be fair, avoiding a view that a mediator might be biased, equalising the position for both parties, and ensuring both parties can mediate in their mother tongue. Secondly, that having a mediator from each State ensures that there is sufficient knowledge of the legal system in both States. However, it is suggested that both these justifications are problematic.

With regard to the first justification mediators are required to be impartial, independent and neutral and as such there should be no need for cultural balance between the mediators and the parties. Indeed, seeking to establish such balance can actually work to the detriment of mediator impartiality by creating the perception that the mediator of the same nationality and/or gender is there to represent the interests of a particular party.[20] It should be remembered that in mediation the parties retain decision-making responsibility and the mediator's role is to manage the process, which should not be affected by his gender or culture. Indeed as Convention mediators should have domestic experience it is highly likely in a globalised world that they have been required to study the influence of culture on mediation in order to pass their domestic training and will have experience of mediating with parents from different cultures.[21] In addition the bi-national co-mediation model usually requires one mediator to have a legal background and one to have a psycho-social background. Again it is argued that these requirements may be unduly onerous and serve little advantage provided mediators are appropriately trained. A finding of the reunite scheme was that, '[f]rom the

[18] ibid.

[19] Swiss legislation (n 5) Art 8, but see discussion at ch 2, III.B.iii.

[20] Questionnaire Responses (ch 1 n 24) Lorraine Filion.

[21] In my practice as a family mediator in Scotland, I have worked with clients from England and Wales, Greece, Ireland, Morocco, Nigeria, Poland, Portugal, Scotland and Venezuela.

parents' perspective . . . the key requirement is the expertise, professionalism and neutrality of the mediators'.[22]

Additionally, a particularly interesting finding of both the 1999 and 2003 Studies was that only a small majority of abducting parents had the nationality of the State of refuge.[23] The assumption that abductors are generally 'going home' is too simplistic. Equally, the assumption that an application involves nationals of the two relevant States is not borne out in data. Therefore where a bi-national model is established with a mediator from each State, a not insignificant number of cases will involve parties who are not respectively nationals of those States. In 43 per cent of mediated cases in the reunite scheme neither parent had the nationality of the State of habitual residence. In 36 per cent of cases neither parent had the nationality of the State of refuge and in 7 per cent of cases neither parent had the nationality of either State.[24]

Regarding the language of mediation, generally parties share at least one common language and may be comfortable to mediate in this language even if it is not their mother tongue. Where parties are bilingual it would certainly be beneficial to use bilingual mediators, however, this does not require a bi-national mediation model. Alternatively, interpreters can be used and it was found in the reunite scheme that '[w]here the use of an interpreter is necessary it does not hinder the mediation process and does not affect the ability to reach a Memorandum of Understanding within the allocated timeframe'.[25]

The second principle underlying the bi-national co-mediation approach is that having a mediator from each State ensures that there is sufficient knowledge of the legal system in both States. In Convention mediation parties are permitted and indeed encouraged to discuss issues which impact upon the child's place of residence; however, the majority of the negotiation will relate to practical arrangements, not legal rights or obligations, which the parties of their own volition cannot alter. The relevant information needed to assist the parties is thus more practical than legal. Information may be needed, inter alia, on the dates of school holidays; the average costs of flights at different times of the year; and provision for language tuition or religious instruction in the local area. In this regard one of the key requirements recognised by the mediators in the reunite scheme was the importance of administrative personnel to make these types of enquiries during the course of mediation.[26] Where detailed legal advice is required to assist the parents' discussions this should be sought from a lawyer or through the Central Authority and fed-back into mediation.[27]

[22] reunite Report (n 3) 52.

[23] 55 per cent in 2003; 52 per cent in 1999, N Lowe, 'A Statistical Analysis of Applications made in 2003 under the Hague Convention of 25 October 1980 on the Civil Aspects of International Child Abduction: Part I: Overall Report' Prel. Doc. No 3/2006 (2007 update) http://hcch.e-vision.nl/upload/wop/abd_pd03e1_2007.pdf 2008 [2003 Study] 23–5.

[24] reunite report (n 3) 14.

[25] ibid 53.

[26] Information from Denise Carter.

[27] While mediators should be able to provide some basic information on the law in each State they are not permitted to offer legal advice, which is rightly left to lawyers.

It is thus submitted that a bi-national model is not necessary in Convention cases. However, it may be a useful first-step as States experiment with developing Convention mediation. Establishing a bi-national scheme can build trust and expertise between the practitioners and authorities in the two States, and enhance processes for recognition and enforcement of mediated agreements which have become court orders.[28] Additionally, allowing States to choose who they partner with can promote the use of mediation between jurisdictions where mediation is well known domestically. Alternatively, a bi-national model may be beneficial where there is a high volume of Convention applications between two particular States. This might be more of a procedural advantage to the State authorities rather than an advantage to the parties because, as already noted, many families involved in Convention applications represent cultures other than those of the relevant States.[29]

Notwithstanding these advantages it is suggested that the first approach highlighted above, whereby mediation takes place in the State of refuge, is far more in keeping with the application of a multilateral Convention as it means that mediation can be available in any incoming case regardless of the State of origin. Moreover, emphasis should be put upon the importance of adequate mediator training which should alleviate any concerns raised by using mediators only from the State of refuge. Additionally, Convention applications are handled by the State of refuge, and establishing mediation within the procedure of that State seems the most appropriate place for the mediation process. However, where mediation takes place through distance telecommunications because the parties are not able to meet in the same State, there is benefit in proceeding with a mediator sitting with each party. In these cases establishing co-operation with colleagues in other States will be imperative, or a mediator from the State of refuge could

[28] Where neither the Convention on Jurisdiction, Applicable Law, Recognition, Enforcement and Co-operation in respect of Parental Responsibility and Measures for the Protection of Children (adopted 19 October 1996, entered into force 1 January 2002) 35 ILM 1391 [1996 Hague Convention] nor Council Regulation (EC) 2201/2003 of 27 November 2003 concerning jurisdiction and the recognition and enforcement of judgments in matrimonial matters and the matters of parental responsibility, repealing Regulation (EC) No 1347/2000 [2003] OJ338/2 [the Brussels II *bis* Regulation] apply. eg, '[t]here is no difficulty in recognition of agreements/orders as between Australia and New Zealand', Questionnaire Responses (ch 1, n 24) Judge Boshier.

[29] The bilateral schemes referred to in this section operate between States with high Convention traffic. In 2003, 35 per cent of applications to Australia were from New Zealand and 67 per cent of applications to New Zealand came from Australia. 85 per cent of applications to Mexico came from the United States and 34 per cent of applications to the United States came from Mexico. 11 per cent of applications to Germany came from the United States and 5 per cent of applications to the United States came from Germany, N Lowe et al, 'A Statistical Analysis of Applications made in 2003 under the Hague Convention of 25 October 1980 on the Civil Aspects of International Child Abduction: Part II: National Reports' Prel. Doc. No 3/2008 (2007 update) http://hcch.evision.nl/upload/wop/abd_pd03ef2007.pdf [2003 Study – National Reports] 16, 213, 295, 321, 481. Additionally, there is an increasing number of abductions between Germany and Poland with 20 cases in 2004 and 42 cases in 2007, S Kiesewetter, 'Emerging Good Practices in the Polish-German Mediation Project' (2009 Strasbourg Conference) (n 2).

travel to the other State.[30] Central Authority co-operation can also assist with the provision of information about the status and nature of mediation in the relevant State.[31]

III. Responding to Specific Challenges

A. Introduction

Establishing a specialist system for Convention mediation can ensure that the process and the practitioners operate within the constraints of the instrument. It also allows for harmonious development of mediation across the range of Contracting States, despite differences at the domestic level. This part of the chapter seeks to illustrate how establishing a special process can address some of the specific challenges raised by mediating within the constraints of the Convention. Particular emphasis is placed on those aspects which would benefit from agreement at the international level.

B. The Scope of Mediation

There is general support for the proposition that Convention mediation must have a broader scope than the Convention court hearing.[32] According to one judge, the benefit of mediation is precisely that it can take other factors into account.[33] Another judge recognised that 'the question of return is not the only problem and often not the real one', and that therefore 'it is not possible to focus only on return' as this decision has 'everything to do with the other aspects' of the situation.[34] It was also stated that the reason there is 'a lot of potential to find a solution via mediation' is because the Convention case is 'never an "end-" decision'.[35] In the reunite scheme all the mediators stated that mediation covered more than the issue of return under the Convention.[36]

Only two questionnaire respondents expressed reluctance for mediation to cover broader issues. One Central Authority noted that 'custody issues are not proper for discussion in cases of abduction',[37] and another stated that 'other issues are specifically excluded as the spirit of the Convention is to speedily return children to their

[30] It is suggested that Central Authorities could provide information on appropriate mechanisms and qualified mediators, possibly accessible via the Hague Conference website.

[31] Convention on the Civil Aspects of International Child Abduction (adopted 25 October 1980, entered into force 1 December 1983) 1343 UNTS 89, Art 7.

[32] Zawid 2008 (n 10) 24–7; Questionnaire Responses (ch 1, n 24); 2006 Responses (n 5) 264–89.

[33] Questionnaire Responses (ch 1, n 24) Judge Schwichtenberg.

[34] ibid, Judge Erb-Klünemann.

[35] ibid, Judge Schwichtenberg.

[36] reunite Report (n 3) 49.

[37] Questionnaire Responses (ch 1, n 24) Maltese Central Authority.

habitual residence where proper investigation can be conducted'.[38] However, both these Central Authorities were interpreting mediation as essentially synonymous with 'voluntary return' and 'amicable resolution'. Both Central Authorities seek to reach a resolution through informal negotiations with the abducting parent, but as these negotiations do not involve the left-behind parent this does not fit the definition of mediation outlined in chapter two.[39] Rather both these authorities quite rightly put forward the view that informal negotiations in the Convention case should take place within the context and scope of the instrument.

Although generally supported, the broader scope of mediation fundamentally alters the Convention regime and therefore is not without its challenges. Three specific issues require discussion to avoid potential problems and encourage broad acceptance. Firstly, questions of jurisdiction and applicable law; secondly, the extent of the scope of Convention mediation; and thirdly, the interaction between mediation and the court process where mediation does not lead to agreement.

With regard to the first point the twofold objectives of the instrument are to 'secure the prompt return' of the abducted child, and to ensure that 'rights of custody and of access under the law of one Contracting State are effectively respected in the other Contracting States'.[40] To this end the authorities in the State of refuge are prohibited from making substantive orders until the Convention application has been dealt with.[41] Against this backdrop, allowing parents to address the substantive issues of their dispute in the course of Convention proceedings in the State of refuge could be seen as contrary to the letter and the spirit of the instrument as it does not guarantee the return of the child and thereby does not necessarily uphold the primacy of the law of the State of habitual residence. However, the Convention does permit and indeed encourage parental agreements and where parents can resolve the issue amicably the Convention application can be dropped and the authorities in the State of refuge are then able to make any necessary substantive orders.[42] However, allowing parents to discuss broader issues in the State of refuge prior to the resolution of the dispute could raise concerns.

These concerns are best addressed by emphasising that in mediation it is the parties themselves who formulate solutions and not the authorities. Therefore while the procedural rules of the State of refuge may be engaged, any agreement is determined by the parties not by the substantive law of the State of refuge. Therefore although issues may arise regarding the jurisdiction of the courts to subsequently make the agreement into a court order,[43] the place where the negotiations take place should not cause any concerns. It is interesting that discussion with those involved in bi-national co-mediation initiatives indicates that the philosophy underlying these projects is not generally concern for the primacy of the

[38] ibid, South African Central Authority.

[39] ch 2, II.C.

[40] Art 1.

[41] Art 16.

[42] E Pérez-Vera, 'Explanatory Report' in *Actes et documents de la quatorzième session, Tome III, Enlèvement d'enfants* (Hague Conference The Hague, 1982) 426 [Explanatory Report] [121].

[43] III.H. below.

State of habitual residence as might have been expected. It is widely recognised that mediation is substantively different from the court process. Parties in general cannot of their own volition alter their legal rights or obligations[44] and therefore in Convention mediation a party cannot lose custody or contact rights, which have been determined by the State of habitual residence; rather, the mediated agreement establishes how those rights and indeed parental responsibilities might be exercised.

The second challenge is how to define the limits of the scope of Convention mediation. The scope is broader than the Convention court hearing yet narrower than the subsequent domestic litigation. The primary focus must be the ultimate place of residence of the child and broader issues which go beyond the scope of the Convention court hearing are admissible in discussion only where they impact upon the parties' ability to make a decision on this primary issue. Deciding which issues are suitable for discussion is the responsibility of the mediator and will depend upon the circumstances of the case.[45] The types of issues which were discussed under the reunite scheme, but which could fall outside the scope of the Convention court hearing included, inter alia, contact, child support, sharing of responsibilities, travel arrangements, financial arrangements and the exchange of information.[46] The fact that these types of issues may fall outside the scope of the Convention court hearing, and if discussed and agreed may only form unenforceable undertakings or conditions attached to a court order, could limit voluntary agreement being reached in court proceedings. However, these issues are ripe for discussion in Convention mediation.

Other issues may necessitate 'proper investigation',[47] for example, the division of property or financial assets. Mediators dealing with such issues usually require additional training as a deeper knowledge of the legal system is needed. This should not be a requirement for Convention mediators whose purpose is to assist parents to make decisions about the child's place of residence. Viewing Convention mediation as part of the broader procedure for handling an application means that it should benefit from any advantageous regime established for Convention cases, such as favourable funding provision, legal representation and expeditious processes. Such advantages can be justified in the Convention context given that the place of residence of the child is not yet decided. However, other matters in dispute, such as property division or divorce, should not necessarily benefit from this regime. It is therefore not the primary aim of Convention mediation to resolve the totality of the dispute, but rather to deal with the child's future place of residence so that any further intervention on other issues is less disruptive to the child.

[44] Directive 2008/52/EC of the European Parliament and of the Council of 21 May 2008 on certain aspects of mediation in civil and commercial matters [Mediation Directive] 'should not apply to rights and obligations on which the parties are not free to decide themselves under the relevant applicable law. Such rights and obligations are particularly frequent in family law' (Recital 10). See also Art 1(2).

[45] In Brazil mediators will allow parents to discuss any issue that they both agree to discuss, including financial issues, Zawid 2008 (n 10) 27.

[46] reunite Report (n 3) 49.

[47] Questionnaire Responses (ch 1, n 24) South African Central Authority.

Another challenge raised by the scope of mediation is that if agreement is not reached the case falls to be resolved in court where the scope is more limited. Other matters pertinent in the quest to reach agreement are no longer relevant and may in fact prejudice a party's case if brought up in court.[48] This highlights the importance of the fact that mediation is confidential and that confidentiality rules are agreed upfront, particularly that participation in mediation cannot be viewed as acquiescence under the Convention.[49] It also underlines the importance of providing adequate information so that parents and professionals are aware of the different scope of the two processes and can act accordingly.[50] The different scope of the two processes also provides support for the idea that certain issues should be viewed in the light of the application itself, not as an element of the mediation or court processes. One example is hearing the child, and the need to avoid a situation where a child would be required to be heard twice under two different processes with two different scopes.[51] The unusual scope of Convention mediation highlights the importance of establishing it as a special scheme so that mediators are aware of the context for mediation.

C. Expeditious Procedures

Contracting States are required to implement the Convention using the 'most expeditious procedures available'.[52] Viewing mediation as part of the broader procedure for handling a Convention application means that the mediation process must also take place under the most expeditious procedures. States have been keen to ensure that 'mediation should not be used if it would delay the prompt return of the child',[53] and where it is used as a delaying tactic it should be terminated.[54] It was recognised in the reunite scheme that 'delaying the Hague process in any substantial way would not be acceptable'.[55]

The requirement to use expeditious procedures has two important implications. Firstly, pathways into and out of mediation must be expeditious; and secondly, the mediation process itself must be contracted within a short timeframe. Expeditious pathways are highly important[56] and it has been stated that, 'in abduction proceed-

[48] In Germany, where the court hearing may have already taken place prior to mediation, this issue would not arise, see ch 2, III.B.ii.

[49] Art 13(1)(a), see III.E below.

[50] ch 2, III.B.iv.

[51] See ch 5, IV.

[52] Art 2.

[53] Recommendation No R(98)1 of the Committee of Ministers to Member States on Family Mediation (adopted by the Committee of Ministers on 21 January 1998) www.coe.int/t/e/legal_affairs/legal_co-operation/family_law_and_children%27s_rights/conferences/Rec(98)1%20E.pdf [Council of Europe Recommendation] VIII(b).

[54] 2006 Responses (n 5) 289 United States; Questionnaire Responses (ch 1, n 24) Austrian Central Authority.

[55] reunite Report (n 3) 7.

[56] 2006 Responses (n 5) 264–89; reunite Report (n 3) 7.

ings, both mediators should be available to conduct mediation preferably within one to two weeks of the assignment'.[57] Additionally, where mediation fails to lead to agreement there must be expeditious pathways into court to resolve the Convention dispute.[58] States have ensured that a case can enter the court process expeditiously by establishing rules allowing filing on the same day the mediation fails,[59] or within 24 hours,[60] or under a summary procedure.[61] If mediation is offered during the court process a simple notification to the court may be all that is required to move the case into the court for a decision.[62] In Germany if the judge has already heard the Convention case[63] he is able immediately to make an order without requiring a further hearing.[64] In the reunite scheme 73 per cent of lawyers representing the applicant parent and 90 per cent of lawyers representing the defendant parent stated that the final hearing was not delayed owing to the mediation.[65]

The need for the mediation process itself to take place expeditiously perhaps represents the most significant difference between general family mediation and Convention mediation. Usual family mediation consists of a few sessions often separated by a few weeks, during which time parents have the opportunity to effectively 'try-out' their arrangements. Small steps might be taken in between sessions which help to allay fears or build trust allowing greater steps to then be taken at a subsequent session. Conversely, Convention mediation typically takes place over a weekend or a few consecutive days.[66] Timeframes may be specified in legislation,[67] or by the court,[68] and may only be extended on agreement of the court and the parties.[69]

[57] Wrocław Declaration on Mediation of Bi-national Disputes over Parents' and Children's Issues (Wroclaw, October 2007) www.bafm-mediation.de/wp-content/uploads/image/images/wroclaw-declaration.pdf. This Declaration resulted from two meetings of German and Polish mediators (Berlin, May 2007) and (Wroclaw, October 2007) [Wroclaw Declaration]. All mediators working for BAFM and its successor organisation (Mediation in international conflicts involving parents and children (MiKK) founded in July 2008 www.mikk-ev.de) follow the principles in the Declaration. A further meeting took place in Viadrina in October 2008 and this declaration is available in German and Polish www.bafm-mediation.de/international/deutsch/deklaracja-viadrina-viadrina-deklaration-15102008/.

[58] Questionnaire Responses (ch 1, n 24) Lord Justice Thorpe; Maltese Central Authority.

[59] ibid, Polish Central Authority.

[60] ibid, Lorraine Filion.

[61] Swiss legislation (n 5) Art 8(2).

[62] Questionnaire Responses (ch 1, n 24) Judge Carl; Judge Olland.

[63] See ch 2, III.B.ii.

[64] Questionnaire Responses (ch 1, n 24) Judge Carl; Judge Schwichtenberg.

[65] Delay was encountered in four cases: One because the parent needed to apply for a passport, another because the parents decided to mediate only seven days before the date of the final hearing, and in the other two cases the delay was caused by difficulty getting flights, reunite Report (n 3) 34, 38.

[66] In the reunite scheme 'three mediation sessions were provided over a 2-day period. Each mediation session lasted a maximum of 3 hours', ibid 11.

[67] See Act on Recognition and Enforcement of Foreign Decisions concerning Custody, etc., and on the Return of Children (1989:14) [Swedish legislation] s 16; Polish Code of Procedural Law Art 183§1 in 2006 Responses (n 5) 282.

[68] Questionnaire Responses (ch 1, n 24) per Judge Carl, 'I have observed that judges have given the parties a deadline of between about 10 days and 3 weeks to carry out the mediation'. Per Judge Boshier, 'Judicial control needs to be tight if proceedings have been filed because speed in completion of applications is important'.

[69] ibid, Judge Erb-Klünemann; New Zealand Central Authority.

Contracting mediation to fit within the Convention timeframe has not appeared to limit its success.[70] One organisation stated that it has 'good experience with mediation sessions concentrated in a short timeframe',[71] and 82 per cent of parents involved in the reunite scheme who responded to a question on the subject, felt that the time period for mediation was long enough.[72] A particular challenge is ensuring that safeguards are not overlooked. The need for speed and expeditious action must not detract from the need for mediation to be a safe and appropriate process. In this regard the intake process is vital and can be expedited through the development of checklists to ensure that parties are fully informed and appropriate safeguards are put in place.[73] Intake sessions can also take place by telephone.[74]

Research reveals that mediation can be commenced expeditiously; the process itself can take place over a period of a few days; and where mediation does not lead to agreement the case can enter the court process on short notice. Where each of these three aspects of the procedure can occur in a matter of days any delay is minimal. One of the key findings of the reunite scheme was 'that mediation does not delay the Hague process in any substantial way'.[75] Indeed, the system was 'sufficiently robust to ensure that, in the main, mediation was undertaken and concluded within' six weeks.[76] The German Central Authority also noted that: 'in the cases we are aware of . . . mediation in Hague Child Abduction cases did not have any influence on the time frame of the Hague Convention'.[77]

While resolving the case within the six-week timeframe is certainly to be commended and must be the aim, it is necessary to be realistic about the current rate at which States deal with Convention applications. Even without an option to mediate very few cases reach resolution in six weeks and therefore the majority of cases are already subject to some delay.[78] It is thus suggested that the important issue should be the avoidance of 'undue delay'. Indeed, two Special Commission meetings have affirmed the use of this terminology in the context of seeking voluntary return or amicable resolution, which 'should not result in any *undue delay* in return proceedings'.[79] Where proceedings face minimal delay due to the media-

[70] Additionally, mediators 'are often asked for a follow-up after some months, emails and telephone calls with both parents after the end of the mediation are usual. And we recommend the mediation to be continued by other mediators at the final place of residence', Paul 2009 (n 2).

[71] Questionnaire Responses (ch 1, n 24) Swiss Foundation of the ISS.

[72] 3 per cent felt it was too long, and 15 per cent not long enough, reunite Report (n 3) 20.

[73] ch 2, II.D.ii.

[74] Questionnaire Responses (ch 1, n 24) Judge Carl; reunite Report (n 3) 10.

[75] reunite Report (n 3) 55.

[76] ibid.

[77] Questionnaire Responses (ch 1, n 24).

[78] 2003 Study (n 23) 45.

[79] 'Conclusions and Recommendations of the Fourth Meeting of the Special Commission to Review the Operation of the Hague Convention of 25 October 1980 on the Civil Aspects of International Child Abduction' (March 2001) http://hcch.evision.nl/upload/concl28sc4_e.pdf [2001 Conclusions] [1.11]; 'Conclusions and Recommendations of the Fifth Meeting of the Special Commission to Review the Operation of the Hague Convention of 25 October 1980 on the Civil Aspects of International Child Abduction and the Practical Implementation of the Hague Convention of 19 October 1996 on Jurisdiction, Applicable Law, Recognition, Enforcement and Co-operation in respect of Parental

tion process, 'the time spent would be worthwhile'.[80] In the 'handful of cases where mediation was not concluded within the six-week period' in the reunite scheme, the 'period of delay was acceptable to the parents and their solicitors, and agreed by the court on the basis that the case was suitable for mediation'.[81] The benchmark should thus be the avoidance of 'undue delay' and an Agreement to Mediate or a preliminary court hearing could specify any circumstances which might allow limited extensions.

The requirement for expeditious proceedings emphasises the importance of creating Convention mediation as a special process. Where cases are referred into the domestic system there are likely to be backlogs, mediators may not be able to adapt their practice to work expeditiously, and the integrity of the process may be compromised.

D. Seising the Court

Under the Convention a delay exists if the authorities have not reached a decision within six weeks of the 'commencement of the proceedings'.[82] Under the Brussels II *bis* Regulation courts are required to issue a judgment 'no later than six-weeks after the application is lodged'.[83] It is therefore important in the context of developing Convention mediation to consider what constitutes the 'commencement of proceedings' and the point at which the application is 'lodged'.

The 'value of initiating mediation prior to judicial procedures or even before the submission of an application'[84] has been noted; however, it is also argued that 'mediation which commenced after judicial proceedings were instituted was more effective, as this created the necessary pressure to speed up the mediation'.[85] In this regard a preliminary ruling can greatly enhance the mediation process by setting out timelines to ensure mediation does not cause undue delay and by putting safeguards in place. In some States to ensure expeditious pathways to court where mediation fails to lead to agreement, it is helpful if the court is already seised prior to the mediation process.[86] In other States seising the court may allow the participants to be eligible for legal aid to pursue mediation.[87]

Responsibility and Measures for the Protection of Children (October–November 2006) www.hcch.net/upload/concl28sc5_e.pdf [2006 Conclusions] [1.3.1] [emphasis added].

[80] Questionnaire Responses (ch 1, n 24) Maltese Central Authority.

[81] reunite Report (n 3) 55.

[82] Art 11(3).

[83] '[E]xcept where exceptional circumstances make this impossible' Art 11(3).

[84] 'Report on the Fifth Meeting of the Special Commission to Review the Operation of the Hague Convention of 25 October 1980 on the Civil Aspects of International Child Abduction and the Practical Implementation of the Hague Convention of 19 October 1996 on Jurisdiction, Applicable Law, Recognition, Enforcement and Co-Operation in respect of Parental Responsibility and Measures for the Protection of Children' (October–November 2006) Prel. Doc. No 19/2007 http://hcch.e-vision.nl/upload/wop/genaff_pd19e2007.pdf [2006 Report] [62].

[85] ibid. See also ch 2, III.B.ii.

[86] Questionnaire Responses (ch 1, n 24) Judge Erb-Klünemann; Judge Olland; Swedish Central Authority.

[87] See III.F below.

Where there is value in having a preliminary ruling prior to commencing mediation the question arises as to whether such a hearing constitutes the commencement of proceedings or the lodging of the application. Where there is no prior ruling the question is whether the commencement of the mediation process should initiate the timeframe. On this second point it has been suggested that time limits 'should not run based on the initiation of mediation on its own'.[88] However, viewing mediation as a part of the procedure for handling the application supports the notion that the mediation process must comply with the timeframe of the instruments. In the context of the Convention provision in Article 11 commencing court proceedings prior to instigating mediation can add great value. It situates mediation squarely within the Convention timeframe and thus encourages expeditious action. Indeed, where mediation was found not to cause delay to the final hearing, this was attributed to the fact that it took place parallel to the court process.[89] The provision in Article 11 of the Convention is essentially aspirational and as such can accommodate mediation which does not cause 'undue delay'.

However, the mandatory provision in Article 11(3) of the Brussels II *bis* Regulation creates difficulties for Convention mediation which proceeds after the application is considered to be lodged. While the Regulation requires Central Authorities to facilitate agreement through mediation,[90] it has been described as 'one of the most anti-mediation pieces of legislation in the canon of family law'.[91] In the specific child abduction context the rigidity of Article 11(3) impacts negatively upon the ability to mediate in these cases. With some notable exceptions European Union States generally fall far short of this provision. In 1999 and 2003 no European Union Member State had an average disposal time which fell within the six-week period.[92] 'More disturbingly, in many Community States, even the fastest disposal times failed to meet the target'.[93] The Mediation Directive, which seeks to encourage the use of mediation within the Union, does not assist as it prevents prescription and limitation periods expiring because of the mediation process but does not deal with the issue of the time limits for handling abduction cases under the Brussels II *bis* Regulation.[94]

[88] 2006 Report (n 84) [63].

[89] 2006 Responses (n 5) 278–83; reunite Report (n 3) 7.

[90] Art 55(e).

[91] D Hodson, 'The EU Mediation Directive: The European Encouragement to Family Law ADR' (2008) *International Family Law* 209 [Hodson 2008] 213. In large part this criticism relates to the jurisdictional rules which encourage a race to issue proceedings and therefore do not favour attempting mediation.

[92] N Lowe and K Horosova, 'The Operation of the 1980 Hague Abduction Convention – A Global View' [2007/2008] 41 *Family Law Quarterly* 59 [Lowe & Horosova 2008] 97. There is no research on disposal times since the Regulation became applicable; however, see K Trimmings, 'The Intra-EU Child Abduction Regime: Necessity or Caprice? Empirical Study of the Effectiveness of Child Abduction Provisions in the Brussels IIbis Regulation. The Added Value of the New Intra-EU Child Abduction Regime', thesis submitted for the award of PhD at the University of Aberdeen, United Kingdom, in 2010.

[93] Lowe & Horosova 2008 (n 92) 97–8.

[94] Art 8. For discussion of the application of this provision in the abduction context see Hodson 2008 (n 91).

It is thus suggested that where the Regulation applies States should think very carefully about seising the court before instigating mediation, or considering the institution of a mediation process to constitute the lodging of the application for the purposes of Article 11(3).[95] Projects in both Germany and in England have demonstrated that mediation can fit within the six-week timeframe;[96] however, the rigidity of the provision suggests that mediation may need to take place prior to the application being lodged. Ironically as a result a provision which intended to speed up disposal of applications could in fact lead to further delay in intra-Union cases. Mediation would still be subject to the requirement to use the 'most expeditious procedures available',[97] but the mediation process would sit outside the six-week timeframe of Article 11(3) of the Brussels II *bis* Regulation. Conversely mediation in non-Union cases would benefit from the encouragement to expeditious action created by including the process within the six-week timeframe of the Convention. Courts are then able to monitor timeframes and keep as the goal the avoidance of undue delay, which seems a more realistic benchmark.

E. Confidentiality

Confidentiality is vital to the success of the mediation process as parties may be unwilling to divulge information or make concessions through negotiation if they believe this could prejudice a future court hearing. At a domestic level the content of mediation is confidential in most States, with the exception of child protection concerns. Only in a minority of jurisdictions (mainly within the United States) can mediators be required to inform the court about the content of mediation, or be called as witnesses.[98] In many States legislation guarantees that mediators have legal privilege.[99] Following the established practice in the majority of States, there is general agreement that the content of Convention mediation should be confidential.[100]

In general, parties in domestic mediation can be assured by legislation or professional codes of conduct that mediators will not divulge the content of discussions; however, the extent to which parties themselves are bound by confidentiality

[95] See also Art 16.

[96] See III.C. above.

[97] Brussels II *bis* Regulation (n 28) Art 11(3); Convention, Art 2.

[98] See 'Feasibility Study on Cross-Border Mediation in Family Matters' Prel. Doc. No 20/2007 www.hcch.net/upload/wop/genaff_pd20e2007.pdf [2007 Feasibility Study] 10.

[99] eg in Scotland under the Civil Evidence (Family Mediation) (Scotland) Act 1995 s 1–2. However, in a recent case outside the family area, it was stated that while a court must recognise that the mediation process needs protection, as with all legal fields principles of privilege and confidentiality have their limits and exceptions, *Farm Assistance Ltd v Secretary of State for the Environment, Food and Rural Affairs (No 2)* [2009] EWHC 1102.

[100] 2007 Feasibility Study (n 98) 9–10; 2006 Report (n 84) [66]; and Questionnaire Responses (ch 1, n 24).

requirements varies. If parties wish to depart from confidentiality requirements they may be able to do so by agreement.[101] Conversely, in some States confidentiality cannot be waived, and may be guaranteed by statute.[102]

The cross-border nature of Convention mediation means that confidentiality must be accepted in both relevant legal systems. An Agreement to Mediate should include a clear clause on the confidentiality of the content of mediation. An agreement on confidentiality can then govern the process notwithstanding that rules may differ in the two relevant States. Any exceptions to confidentiality must be made known to the parties upfront. The following is an example of a confidentiality clause in a child abduction Agreement to Mediate:

> (a) All information and correspondence from either of you is shared with you both. As mediators, we cannot receive any information or correspondence on a confidential basis from one of you, without sharing it with the other. (b) We would be glad if you would agree that, in the event of contested court proceedings taking place, neither of you would call us to give evidence in court.[103] (c) We treat the content of our discussions and the information you provide as confidential. We will not provide information to legal advisers or to any other third party, except at the written request of both parties.[104]

Where parties reach agreement in mediation they will, however, be encouraged to speak to their lawyers with a view to having the proposed agreement drawn up as a court order.[105] Therefore it should be understood upfront that confidentiality exists unless and until an agreement is reached. In the reunite scheme:

> It was emphasised during the mediation process that the Memorandum of Understanding could not be treated as: (a) a completed and binding agreement in child abduction proceedings; or (b) disclosable in child abduction proceedings; or (c) constitute acquiescence pursuant to article 13(a) unless and until it had been submitted as a consent order in Hague proceedings.[106]

Conversely, where mediation does not lead to agreement the content of mediation remains confidential and mediators should not be called as witnesses in court. Statements made in mediation with a view to reaching an agreement should not prejudice a party's Convention application in court and therefore must be inadmissible. Equally, a court should draw no inference from a party's willingness or unwillingness to enter into mediation.[107]

[101] Questionnaire Responses (ch 1, n 24) Judge Carl.

[102] eg Art 815.3 of the Code of Civil Procedure in Quebec Canada, Questionnaire Responses (ch 1, n 24) Lorraine Filion; Art 183.4 § 2 of the Polish Code of Civil Procedure, 2006 Responses (n 5) 275.

[103] In this context the mediators did not benefit from a statutory legal privilege and therefore requested that the parties agreed not to call them as witnesses.

[104] BAFM Agreement to Mediate www.bafmmediation.de/International/english/agreement-to-mediate/ [BAFM Agreement to Mediate].

[105] Conversely, if parties choose not to have their agreement made into an enforceable order it remains confidential between them.

[106] reunite Report (n 3) 9; see also Mediation Directive (n 44) Art 7(1)(b).

[107] In some common law countries an Agreement to Mediation needs a clause which guarantees that the participation in mediation is without prejudice to subsequent legal proceedings, Paul 2009 (n 2).

When Convention mediation was first being considered there was a general concern that if the applicant consented to mediate, a court may interpret this as acquiescence,[108] thus prejudicing the outstanding return application.[109] Happily in practice this has not proved to be a problem.[110] One respondent to the Questionnaire noted that as mediation is initiated by the court the issue is not relevant.[111] In another State the Supreme Court has confirmed that temporary agreement does not hinder a later request for a return order.[112] Judges from the civil law tradition have stated that the issue is of more concern in common law jurisdictions[113] and in order to accommodate 'problems arising in Anglo-Saxon legal practice in particular, a special clause has been developed' in Germany:

> if prior to the substantive court hearing of the application, the parties agree to attempt to resolve the issues between them (or some of those issues) through mediation, nothing said or done by either party agreeing to make such an attempt or in the course of the mediation will be admissible in evidence herein (whether as evidence of acquiescence on the part of the plaintiff or otherwise); and that the court will draw no inference about the strength or otherwise of a party's case in the proceedings from his or her agreement to make such an attempt.[114]

In the reunite scheme 'it was emphasised to both parents that mediation could only be undertaken with the full consent of both parents and an unwillingness to enter into mediation would not have an effect on the outcome of the Hague application'.[115] While it appears that States have not interpreted agreement to attempt mediation as acquiescence for Convention purposes, asking parties to agree to a clause similar to that stated above removes any concern. The cross-border nature of the dispute and the involvement of two legal systems means that agreements on confidentiality must be recognised in both States and lawyers can be asked to confirm this.[116]

F. Costs and Sources of Funding

Applications under the Convention are essentially free of charge to the applicant.[117] However, States are permitted to make a reservation such that they are not bound to assume any costs 'resulting from the participation of legal counsel or advisers or from court proceedings, except insofar as those costs may be covered

[108] Art 13(1)(a).
[109] reunite Report (n 3) 7.
[110] Questionnaire Responses (ch 1, n 24).
[111] ibid, Swedish Central Authority.
[112] ibid, Austrian Central Authority citing law OGH 5 Ob 17/08y.
[113] ibid, Judge Carl; Judge Olland.
[114] BAFM Agreement to Mediate (n 104).
[115] reunite Report (n 3) 9.
[116] Further thought may need to be given to the important issue of confidentiality if practice reveals a need for tighter rules.
[117] Art 26.

by its system of legal aid and advice'.[118] Just under half of the Contracting States have made such a reservation.[119] Establishing mediation as an aspect of the broader procedure for handling a case means that the same advantageous scheme might be available for costs associated with mediation.[120]

As a voluntary alternative to the court hearing, States should not be required to provide free mediation; however, incorporating mediation within the procedure for handling an application suggests that wherever possible it should be free to the applicant. Indeed, if Convention mediation is to develop as a viable alternative to the court hearing it must be cost effective to the parties and to the State. Where a State has made a reservation but has a legal aid system it might be possible to establish Convention mediation in such a way that participants can receive legal aid to mediate. In some States where a mediation process is annexed to the courts or if the court has been seised,[121] participants are eligible for legal aid.[122] Even where public funding is not available for domestic family mediation it may be possible to make funding available in Convention cases justified by the extra disruption caused by the cross-border nature of the dispute. Additionally, it should be remembered that the number of cases is small. Across the globe there were only 1259 applications captured by the 2003 Study.[123] Only five States received more than 50 applications and over 70 per cent of States received less than 15 applications while 24 per cent received no applications at all.[124] Viewed in these terms the real costs to the State of providing free mediation in these cases is small.

The reunite scheme identified the cost of Convention mediation and broke down the different components. Typical costs were £2640,[125] and lawyers supporting the mediation process incurred average costs of £271.[126] Without a comparative analysis of costs of the Convention court hearing it is hard to evaluate the cost-effectiveness of mediation. However, the costs associated with mediation should be viewed against the broader backdrop that parties may resolve the majority of their dispute, negating the need for subsequent litigation. Such litigation being domestic in nature does not fall within the often financially advantageous Convention regime.

118 Art 26(3).

119 40 out of the 84 States: www.hcch.net/Index_en.php?act=conventions.status&cid=24. The United Kingdom made a reservation but did not implement it so that all applicants are provided with free legal representation regardless of means or merits.

120 Swiss legislation (n 5) Art 14 expressly states that Art 26 applies to costs of mediation proceedings. (Switzerland has not made a reservation to Art 26.)

121 Questionnaire Responses (ch 1, n 24) New Zealand Central Authority; Note on the Development of Mediation (n 11) 19.

122 In England and Wales the Legal Services Commission provides funding for mediation, National Audit Office, 'Legal Services Commission: Legal Aid and Mediation for People Involved in Family Breakdown' HC 256 Session 2006–07 (March 2007) www.nao.org.uk [Legal Services Commission Report].

123 2003 Study (n 23) 8.

124 ibid 9, 13. The United Kingdom is here considered as one State despite being analysed separately in the Study.

125 reunite Report (n 3) 51.

126 These costs included a range from no cost at all to £750. Given the broad range it is helpful to outline that the median average was £200, ibid 33, 38.

Therefore Convention mediation may reduce the overall costs to the parties and to the States.[127] While 'demonstrating that mediation can reduce legal costs is notoriously difficult, experience . . . indicates that contested children applications [are] avoided and agreements reached [are] satisfactory to all'.[128] Against this backdrop anecdotal evidence has shown that parties are often willing to pay for Convention mediation.[129] However, ensuring adequate funding is vital to the success of mediation.

G. Distance Telecommunications

It is widely acknowledged that Convention mediation should preferably take place in the State of refuge with both parents face-to-face.[130] This causes less disruption to the child and enables contact between the child and the left-behind parent in appropriate cases. Interestingly, allowing contact has been thought to be instrumental in affecting decisions. In one case contact enabled the left-behind father to 'see how well the mother had kept and educated his daughter'.[131] The implication was that this reduced conflict and improved communication. Equally, as a result of allowing contact with the left-behind parent 'sometimes the abducting parent feels that he/she has made a mistake'.[132] Contact during the course of mediation has 'led to a better negotiation atmosphere between the parents in the further course of mediation'[133] and is a way to 'lower the conflict', lower 'the fears' and 'focus on the child'.[134]

One mediation provider stated that establishing contact during mediation is one of the 'central issues' of its work[135] and another noted that contact 'might even be a condition for success in some cases'.[136] It is therefore suggested that further work should be done on supporting contact between a child and a parent who has come to the State of refuge for the purposes of mediation. In some States the court can either encourage or order contact to take place.[137] In other States contact might be negotiated between the parents at the outset of the mediation process.

While there are benefits to mediating with both parents in the State where the child is, in Convention cases this is not always possible. The left-behind parent may not have the appropriate documentation to be able to enter the State of

[127] 'Explanatory Memorandum to Recommendation No R(98)1 of the Committee of Ministers to Member States on Family Mediation' [Council of Europe Memorandum] [7].

[128] L Parkinson, 'Child-inclusive Family Mediation' (2006) *Family Law* 483 [Parkinson 2006] 487.

[129] This has been the experience of the reunite mediators, information from Denise Carter.

[130] Questionnaire Responses (ch 1, n 24).

[131] ibid, BAFM.

[132] ibid, Judge Schwichtenberg.

[133] ibid, Judge Carl.

[134] ibid, Swiss Foundation of the International Social Service.

[135] ibid, BAFM.

[136] ibid, Swiss Foundation of the International Social Service.

[137] eg in Germany, s 38(2) of the German Act on International Family Law Proceedings.

refuge for the purposes of participating in mediation.[138] Additionally, 'economic limitations of the majority of families involved in these disputes dictate that mediation will occur through video teleconference'.[139] In a few cases Convention mediation has proceeded with parties in different States using distance telecommunications, such as the Internet, video or teleconferencing facilities, or simply the telephone. American mediators in larger cities have used telephonic equipment in embassies and consulates and are pursuing contacts with businesses and law firms which might be willing to donate facilities.[140] The use of distance telecommunications to facilitate cross-border mediation is explicitly mentioned in the Mediation Directive,[141] and it is to be assumed that this area will develop rapidly.

In principle the same rules should apply to mediation regardless of the medium through which it occurs. Parents can be required to sign an Agreement to Mediate which will specify, inter alia, confidentiality requirements. Mediating through distance telecommunications will certainly require the co-operation of mediators and Central Authorities in the two States. It may be preferable to proceed with one mediator present with each party. An alternative option was used in the reunite scheme where a mediator spoke to one client on the phone while another mediator spoke to the other client. The mediators then spoke to each other and subsequently relayed information back to the parties.[142] While mediation conducted via telecommunications may be less satisfactory for parties and mediators, there should be no reason in principle why it could not be beneficial in these cases.[143] As this area remains novel further research is needed. Some assistance can be gained from recent efforts in the growing field of Online Dispute Resolution (ODR).[144]

H. Enforceability

Mediated agreements are by nature non-binding,[145] and one of the perceived benefits of mediation is precisely the fact that parties may prefer to retain a certain degree of flexibility and lack of formality in the organisation of their family affairs.

[138] eg a left-behind parent who is not a national of a State within the United States' visa-waiver program, would not be able expeditiously to get a visa to enter the United States for the purposes of mediation, information from Julia Alanen.

[139] 2006 Responses (n 5) 278 United States.

[140] Such methods are not readily available in more rural locations.

[141] Recital 9.

[142] reunite Report (n 3) 14.

[143] Questionnaire Responses (ch 1, n 24) Judge Boshier.

[144] For discussion see Zawid 2008 (n 10) 33.

[145] However, in Sweden 'an agreement on custody and contact . . . is valid, and thus enforceable, in Sweden if it is in writing and the social welfare committee approves it in accordance with Chapter 6 Section 6 and Section 15a of the Children and Parents Code (1949:381). The social welfare committee shall approve the agreement if it is not manifestly incompatible with the best interests of the child'. Parties can ask the court to make an agreement into an order for the purposes of enforceability in the other jurisdiction, Questionnaire Responses (ch 1, n 24) Swedish Central Authority.

Additionally, one of the recognised benefits of mediation over litigation is that parties are more likely to adhere to agreed arrangements, reducing the need for subsequent enforcement.[146] On the other hand, parties may opt not to mediate if mediation is 'regarded as a poorer alternative to judicial proceedings in the sense that compliance with agreements resulting from mediation would depend on the good will of the parties'.[147] The Council of Europe Recommendation also recognises the importance of establishing structures to facilitate approval and enforcement of mediated agreements.[148]

There must be mechanisms available to give effect to a mediated agreement if the parties so desire. Having such mechanisms will become mandatory within the European Union when the Mediation Directive is transposed into domestic law,[149] and as a result focus in this section is largely on the European Union context. However, at the outset it must be stated that the Mediation Directive only applies in disputes where 'at least one of the parties is domiciled or habitually resident in a Member State other than that of any other party'[150] which may not be the case in a Convention application. However, the Directive additionally states that 'nothing should prevent Member States from applying such provisions also to internal mediation processes'[151] which may mean that States expand the scope in transposition, and any mechanisms created for enforceability could nonetheless be used.

Given the cross-border nature of Convention mediation parties should be encouraged to have their agreements made enforceable. In order to become enforceable agreements generally require to be drawn up as contracts, authentic instruments or court orders.[152] In the family context and the Convention context specifically it is suggested that the most efficient and appropriate mechanism through which a mediated agreement can be given effect is by court order. This also fits with the notion of viewing mediation as part of the procedure for handling a Convention application given that the alternative is the court process and in some cases the court will already be seised. Certainly using the court process to make agreements enforceable has been the favoured option to date in Convention mediation.[153] The vast majority of Questionnaire respondents highlighted that parties in mediation would be encouraged to discuss potential agreements with their legal representative who can then assist in drawing up the agreement in appropriate terms upon which the court can grant a consent order.[154]

In the reunite scheme an agreement was reduced to a Memorandum of Understanding and then drawn up into a consent order. 'Particular attention was

146 2007 Feasibility Study (n 98) 10.
147 Mediation Directive (n 44) Recital 19.
148 Art IV.
149 Art 6(1).
150 Art 2(1).
151 Recital 8.
152 2007 Feasibility Study (n 98) 10–11; Mediation Directive (n 44) Art 6(2).
153 See Note on the Development of Mediation (n 11); Questionnaire Responses (ch 1, n 24); Feasibility Study Responses (n 10).
154 Feasibility Study Response (n 10) 10 Brazil; Questionnaire Responses (ch 1, n 24).

paid to ensure the Memorandum of Understanding, and subsequent order, was sufficiently formed and sufficiently specific to avoid unnecessary future litigation'.[155] A Central Authority noted that part of the agreement process is making sure that what is agreed is in accordance with the law of both States and can be enforceable. Subsequently a memorandum would be 'drafted and signed by parties and counsel seeking orders in the terms specified'.[156]

In order to become an enforceable court order, specific legal requirements may need to be fulfilled such as hearing the child and ensuring the agreement is in the child's best interest.[157] This could add particular value in the Convention context. Generally in mediation there is no obligation upon parents to act in the best interests of the child or in line with his rights, as the dispute remains in the private realm of the family. However, in the Convention case where the court is seised to make the agreement into an order, thought will need to be given to the interests of the child. As the agreement may lead to a child living in a different State to one of his parents, which has serious implications, the ability of the court to assess whether the interests of the child have been sufficiently taken into account offers some extra protection.[158] Certain arrangements may also need prior approval by the court in order to be enforceable.[159] The Directive states that 'the content of an agreement shall be made enforceable' unless it is either 'contrary to the law of the Member State where the request is made or the law of that Member State does not provide for its enforceability'.[160] It is important that the agreement is first made enforceable in the State where it was concluded as the Directive 'should not encourage the parties to circumvent the law of that Member State by having their agreement made enforceable in another Member State'.[161]

In the Convention context a court order made on the basis of a mediated agreement is not a Convention court order per se, rather the court would make a consent order and dismiss the Convention application. If the agreement is for the child's return it may involve additional conditions mutually agreed by the parties which may be beyond the scope of a Convention return order. Conversely an agreement that the child will remain in the State of refuge is not a non-return order under the Convention as such an order is only permissible if one of the limited exceptions to return is made out.[162] Not being a Convention court order, however, raises the question of the legal basis upon which the court in the State of refuge is able to make the order.

Under the provisions of both the 1996 Hague Convention and the Brussels II *bis* Regulation in the case of wrongful removal or retention of a child the State of

[155] reunite Report (n 3) 9.
[156] Questionnaire Responses (ch 1, n 24) New Zealand Central Authority.
[157] ibid, Austrian Central Authority.
[158] ch 4, II.D.
[159] Questionnaire Responses (ch 1, n 24) Judge Carl.
[160] Art 6(2).
[161] Recital 21.
[162] This also means that the provisions of the Brussels II *bis* Regulation (n 28) Art 11(6)–(8) can be avoided preventing a party from subsequently seeking return via this process.

habitual residence retains jurisdiction 'until the child has acquired a habitual residence in another (Member) State and each person . . . having rights of custody has acquiesced in the removal or retention'.[163] Thus for the courts of the State of refuge to have jurisdiction to make a parental responsibility order, the child must have acquired habitual residence in that State and the left-behind parent must have acquiesced.[164] Where the agreement involves the child remaining these conditions can generally be established. Alternatively, where parties agree to the child remaining in the State of refuge the removal or retention could be recategorised as a subsequently agreed relocation and thus not a 'wrongful' removal. Additionally, such a recategorisation avoids the continuing jurisdiction of the original State of habitual residence in the European context if the applicant parent accepts the jurisdiction of the new State of habitual residence.[165]

Where the agreement involves the return of the child courts in the State of refuge might claim jurisdiction on the basis of Article 12(3) of the Brussels II *bis* Regulation. This provision requires the child to have a 'substantial connection'[166] with the State. Certain examples are given which may be fulfilled in a specific case but there will be cases where these criteria are not met. However, according to the Practice Guide, '[t]hese conditions are not exclusive, and it is possible to base the connection on other criteria'.[167] The Regulation purportedly seeks to promote mediated agreements,[168] and indeed ensures their enforceability throughout the Union if they are enforceable in the State in which they were concluded.[169] It would therefore be a strange result to allow agreements to be enforceable and judgments to be enforceable but not to allow agreements to be made into judgments as a means of ensuring their enforceability, where it is the express wish of the parties, on the basis of a lack of jurisdiction.

Under the 1996 Hague Convention a court in the State of refuge could base jurisdiction on Article 11 by which the State where the child is present can take necessary measures of protection in cases of urgency. The term 'urgency' was deliberately left undefined in the Convention[170] and therefore could arguably be broad enough to cover the present situation where, notwithstanding that the child is habitually resident in a State he is about to be returned to, the parents wish to formalise an agreement made in the State where the child is present which specifies aspects of the return. Such measures lapse on return to the State of habitual residence as soon as authorities there make appropriate orders.[171] Therefore to avoid the situation where after return the left-behind parent reneges on the agreement and seises the court,

[163] The 1996 Hague Convention (n 28) Art 7; the Brussels II *bis* Regulation (n 28) Art 10.

[164] For discussion of acquiescence under Art 13(1)(a) of the Convention, see III.E above.

[165] Art 9(2).

[166] Art 12(3)(a).

[167] 'Practice Guide for the application of the new Brussels II Regulation' http://ec.europa.eu/justice_home/doc_centre/civil/doc/parental_resp_ec_vdm_en.pdf 17.

[168] Art 55(e).

[169] Art 46.

[170] P Lagarde, 'Explanatory Report' in *Actes et documents de la dix-huitième session, Tome II, Protection des enfants* (The Hague, Hague Conference, 1996) 514 [Lagarde Report] [567].

[171] Art 11(2).

the original order should be registered or mirrored in the State of habitual residence prior to return.

The ability of the court in the State of refuge to formalise an agreed return is an important advantage of Convention mediation. Currently, where parents might agree or the court might require various conditions to be met to ensure that return is safe these issues are attached to the return order as unenforceable undertakings. While there is often encouragement to have these conditions mirrored in the State of habitual residence, the lack of an enforceable court order threatens their usefulness. If Convention mediation is to add value to the current situation, the content of an agreement on return must be able to be formulated into an enforceable court order.[172]

In addition to being enforceable as a court order in the State where the agreement was concluded, this order must also be enforceable in the other State. This is one of the key goals of the Directive,[173] which relies upon other European instruments to ensure enforceability, in the present context the Brussels II *bis* Regulation. Under this Regulation a judgment shall be recognised in the other Member States without any special procedure being required,[174] and a mediated agreement which has been made into a court order would constitute a 'judgment' for the purposes of these provisions.[175] In the global context the 1996 Hague Convention also has provision to the effect that an order made in one State is in principle enforceable in another State by operation of law.[176] An 'interested party' can also request that the competent authorities in another Contracting State decide in advance whether an order will be recognised.[177] Broader adherence to this instrument will thus benefit Convention mediation.[178]

Where neither the Brussels II *bis* Regulation nor the 1996 Hague Convention applies, a court order could be registered in the other State or a mirror order sought. In the reunite scheme once a court order was drafted, where appropriate, it was registered in the overseas jurisdiction. A German judge stated that he is aware of 'a total of four cases of mirroring an order of this kind and one case of registering a German court order'.[179] Another German judge had experience of signing two mirror orders from the United Kingdom.[180] Interestingly, no respondents to the Questionnaire were aware of any agreements which had required enforcement. While this should be viewed in the context of the fact that to date there are not many Convention mediations, and notwithstanding the importance

[172] See ch 4, II.C.
[173] Recital 20.
[174] Art 28.
[175] Arts 2(4) and 46.
[176] Arts 26–28.
[177] Art 24.
[178] At the time of writing there are 29 Contracting States to this Convention http://hcch.e-vision.nl/index_en.php?act=conventions.status&cid=70. All the European Union Member States had committed to ratification by 5 June 2010, Decision of the Council of the European Union OJ 2008 L151/36.
[179] Questionnaire Responses (ch 1, n 24) Judge Carl.
[180] ibid, Judge Schwichtenberg.

of establishing mechanisms for enforcement, it is assumed that agreements are more likely to be adhered to than court ordered solutions.[181]

I. Training and Qualifications of Mediators

The term 'mediator' is largely unprotected meaning that the requisite training and qualification differs enormously from one State to another, and in some States no training is required. The Mediation Directive is weak regarding both the definition of mediator and the provisions on ensuring the quality of mediation.[182] In part this is because the Directive has a broader scope than just family mediation and it is generally recognised that the subject matter may affect the training and qualification required of mediators.[183] The Uniform Mediation Act similarly says nothing on mediator qualifications. However, it is emphasised that:

> The decision . . . against prescribing qualifications should not be interpreted as a disregard for the importance of qualifications. Rather, respecting the unique characteristics that may qualify a particular mediator for a particular mediation, the silence of the Act reflects the difficulty of addressing the topic in a uniform statute that applies to mediation in a variety of contexts.[184]

An advantage of establishing a special procedure for Convention mediation is that additional training can be required for Convention mediators.[185] Firstly, Convention mediators must be qualified in their State and thus protected by and working within any necessary domestic regulation. Secondly, it is widely agreed that mediators in international cases require additional training.[186] Convention mediators should also be subject to supervision. The Council of Europe Recommendation noted that 'taking into account the particular nature of international mediation, international mediators should be required to undergo specific training'.[187] In the Convention context the particular nuances of the instrument require that 'any mediator undertaking mediation in this type of case has expertise in the field of international parental child abduction and the . . . Convention'.[188] Additionally, Convention mediators need 'a good understanding

[181] J Kelly, 'Family Mediation Research: Is There Empirical Support for the Field?' (2004) 22 *Conflict Resolution Quarterly* 3 [Kelly 2004] 28.

[182] Arts 3 and 4.

[183] Additionally, the Directive must be implemented by 2011, and it is perhaps right to set a low benchmark at this stage.

[184] Uniform Mediation Act drafted by the National Conference of Commissioners on Uniform State Laws 2001 (last revised or amended in 2003) [42].

[185] Mediators working for BAFM and MiKK are obliged to have attended at least one further training course on mediating international conflicts involving parents and children.

[186] Paul 2009 (n 2); M Kleim, 'The work of the European Parliament Mediation Office' (2009 Strasbourg Conference); A Mouttet 'Une formation européenne de qualité adaptée aux spécificités de la médiation familiale internationale' (2009 Strasbourg Conference); Hodson 2008 (n 91).

[187] Art VIII(e).

[188] reunite Report (n 3) 52.

of cultural diversity'.[189] In bi-national co-mediation it is additionally considered that mediators must be 'flexible and willing to cooperate with a mediator from another country . . . and be able to communicate in a foreign language'.[190]

It would be helpful if the necessary additional training was standardised and agreed to ensure quality across jurisdictions. These standards should be agreed at the international level to promote harmony and mutual trust:

> We do not need an Anglo-Saxon system or a Latin system or a Nordic system: we need to incorporate different systems, agree equivalences and develop a standard for international family mediation.[191]

It has been suggested that '[m]ediation advocates working in this field could formulate their *own set* of standards governing both the qualifications and conduct of mediators who are asked to mediate international child abduction cases'.[192] Certainly, mediators should be involved in the process of developing standards. In this regard, reunite developed a training module for its mediators which it has sought to share with mediators in other States. Additionally, in some projects Convention mediators are required to adhere to written rules which can be beneficial in ensuring quality.[193] While there is broad agreement that Convention mediators require additional training, efforts need to be made to harmonise the work that has been done and reach mutually agreed minimum standards. There is also a need for discussion at the State level rather than allowing mediators to purely self-regulate.

There have been several suggestions that a register of mediators 'qualified' to work on these cases should be established.[194] For such a register to be beneficial in ensuring quality, agreement must first be made on appropriate training standards. Offering registers to which mediators can designate themselves with no formal checks could be damaging and allow mediators to circumvent the requisite training. An additional advantage of a register of mediators is that these mediators can be required to submit reports, attend supervision and take part in continued professional training to maintain their place on the register. The register can also note language and other relevant abilities so that appropriate mediators can be easily found. This can help to ensure a high quality of mediators for these complex cases and can ensure expeditious access to a mediator as there is a central point of contact.

Practice to date in Convention mediation has largely involved a co-mediation model where two mediators work together. Given the complexities of these cases

[189] Paul 2009 (n 2), see also ch 2, n 69.
[190] ibid.
[191] Parkinson 2009 (n 3).
[192] Zawid 2008 (n 10) 32 [emphasis in original].
[193] eg, the Wroclaw Declaration (n 57).
[194] Parkinson 2009 (n 3); 'A register of trained and competent mediators for such cases should be compiled and made readily available to the judiciary in each participating state' (International Family Justice Judicial Conference for Common Law and Commonwealth Jurisdictions, Windsor, England, August 2009) [2009 Windsor Conference] conclusions and resolutions [7]. The organisation GEMME (European Association of Judges for mediation) has put together such a list www.gemme.eu/en/.

it has been suggested that they 'should always be co-mediated'[195] and that co-mediators can model behaviours to parents.[196] While the involvement of two mediators does have cost implications, the Wroclaw Declaration states that 'this is justified' because 'in mediation proceedings, in addition to return, questions of parental custody, contact, and other issues . . . can be resolved'[197] and these resolutions are more sustainable, thus saving costs in the longer term. Other experience has shown that the use of two mediators is unnecessary.[198] Different views may reflect different domestic practice and the particular circumstances of the case may dictate whether one or two mediators would be beneficial. If a mediator is used to working solo on complex cases and is subject to regular supervision, there should be no bar in principle to solo mediation unless there is evidence to indicate that outcomes are less satisfactory for families.[199]

In most bi-national co-mediation models one mediator is required to be male and one female; one from a psycho-social background and one with legal training. It is suggested that such a model is unnecessarily cumbersome and that emphasis should rather be placed on mediator training.[200] Many mediators are dual-qualified, for example, as lawyers; however, this can actually create difficulties as it is essential that a mediator acts as a mediator and does not seek to go beyond this role.[201] Mediators should not give legal advice and parties in Convention mediation are usually encouraged to instruct legal representatives. Consequently, Convention mediators should not be required to be lawyers,[202] counsellors or therapists, but simply well-trained mediators. Emphasis should be placed on establishing training standards; training mediators to these standards; and subsequently registering them to work on these cases.

In addition to ensuring appropriate training for mediators, Central Authorities, judges and lawyers require training to familiarise themselves with the mediation process. Depending upon the procedure in the particular State, it may be the responsibility of any one or more of these professionals to refer parties to mediation. They thus need adequate information about what the mediation process is and how it fits within the broader procedure for handling a Convention application. An advantage of viewing mediation as one aspect of this broader procedure means that various Convention professionals can support and assist each other. A degree of interdisciplinary training will be beneficial in this regard to disseminate knowledge and also build working relationships and pathways between relevant professionals.

[195] reunite Report (n 3) 52.

[196] Information from Julia Alanen.

[197] Wroclaw Declaration (n 57).

[198] Questionnaire Responses (ch 1, n 24) Judge Boshier; Lorraine Filion.

[199] There is anecdotal evidence that solo Convention mediation has been successful, information from Melissa Kucinski.

[200] 18 per cent of participants in the reunite scheme stated that having mediators of both sexes present would have been beneficial while 45 per cent did not think mediators of both sexes were needed, reunite Report (n 3) 20. See also discussion at II.B. above.

[201] Mediation Directive (n 44) Art 3(a).

[202] reunite Report (n 3) 52; for a contrary view see Hodson 2008 (n 91) and Questionnaire Response (ch 1, n 24) Judge Boshier.

IV. Conclusion

This chapter focused on the question 'how can a mediation process fit within the constraints of the Convention?' It was stressed that Convention mediation is significantly different from more general family mediation and should thus be viewed as a distinct discipline. Viewing mediation in this way allows the process and the practitioners to adapt to meet various legal, procedural and practical challenges raised by mediating within the constraints of the instrument. Particular emphasis was placed on those issues which would benefit from agreement at the international level. By providing an outline it is hoped that this chapter will encourage further discussion with a view to greater use of mediation in Convention cases.

4

Why Mediate in Convention Cases?

I. Introduction

The previous chapters have focused on what mediation is and how it can fit within the constraints of the Convention. Having established that mediation can operate in Convention cases the question remains, why mediate given the existence of the Convention regime? This chapter seeks to promote a greater use of mediation in Convention cases by highlighting how it can add value to the current regime. Support for the use of Convention mediation essentially stems from two convictions. Firstly, that mediation can address some of the current concerns regarding the operation of the Convention in the present day; and secondly, that mediation as a discipline is particularly beneficial where parties intend to have some degree of ongoing relationship, which is almost always true in parental disputes concerning children. The first and most substantial part of this chapter addresses the first conviction. The second part addresses the benefits inherent in the discipline and the wider added value of mediation. By focusing on the added value of mediation in these cases this chapter seeks to highlight why Convention mediation justifies the resources necessary for its development.

II. Responding to Concerns Surrounding the Operation of the Convention

A. Background and Context

Discussion of how mediation adds value to the Convention regime happily takes place against the backdrop of broad support for the instrument.[1] However, there are a number of concerns regarding the operation of the instrument in the present day. To understand these concerns it is instructive briefly to consider the historical basis upon which the Convention was founded.[2] The phenomenon of interna-

[1] See ch 1, III.

[2] For more detailed analysis see P Beaumont and P McEleavy, *The Hague Convention on International Child Abduction* (Oxford, Oxford University Press, 1999) [Beaumont & McEleavy].

tional child abduction was debated in a number of fora in the 1970s. Discussion at the Council of Europe led to a Convention on the recognition and enforcement of custody decisions, but it did not adequately address the issue of child abduction per se.[3] The subject was also discussed by the Commonwealth nations which opted to follow discussion at the Hague Conference rather than taking a separate stance.[4] The work of the latter organisation culminated in the Convention which was completed in 1980 and entered into force in 1983.[5]

The framers of the Convention benefited from a number of documents providing constructive information on the factual circumstances believed to befall abduction. Empirical research was limited but two formative issues illuminated in this documentation are of particular importance in understanding the ethos of the Convention. Firstly, the belief that abductors were generally non-custodial[6] fathers[7] removing children from their primary carer mothers;[8] and secondly, that 'abduction of children is contrary to their interest and welfare'.[9] While there was significant evidence for both these propositions, there were also dissenting voices.[10] However, these general views prevailed and encouraged the drafters to provide a mechanism which would protect children by deterring the perceived 'evil'[11] of abduction:

> The Convention as a whole rests upon the unanimous rejection of this phenomenon of illegal child removals and upon the conviction that the best way to combat them at an international level is to refuse to grant them legal recognition.[12]

[3] Convention on Recognition and Enforcement of Decisions concerning Custody of Children and on Restoration of Custody of Children of 20 May 1980 (adopted 20 May 1980, entered into force 1 September 1983) ETS No 105.

[4] For a more thorough explanation see A Anton, 'The Hague Convention on International Child Abduction' (1981) 30 *ICLQ* 537 [Anton 1981].

[5] The issue of 'legal kidnapping' had first arisen on the agenda of the organisation in October 1976 *Actes et documents de la treizième session, Tome I, Matières diverses* (Hague Conference, The Hague, 1978) [169–72].

[6] 3 per cent of abducting parents had a custody order in their favour, compared with 39 per cent of left-behind parents. However, in 40 per cent of cases no order had been made, possibly because many of the parents were still married at the time of the abduction, International Social Service, 'Summary of Findings on a Questionnaire Studied by ISS' Prel. Doc. No 3/1979 [ISS Report] in *Actes et documents de la quatorzième session, Tome III, Enlèvement d'enfants* (Hague Conference, The Hague, 1982) [*Actes et documents* 1982].

[7] 76 per cent of abductors surveyed by the International Social Service were fathers, ibid [134]. The preponderance of father abductors was backed up by other contemporaneous research (71 per cent, 76 per cent and 75 per cent), see respectively, M Agopian, *Parental Child Stealing* (Lexington, Lexington Books, 1981); R Janvier, K McCormick and R Donaldson, 'Parental Kidnapping: A Survey of Left Behind Parents' (1990) 41 *Juvenile and Family Court Journal* 1; D Finkelhor, G Hotaling and A Sedlak, 'Children Abducted by Family Members: A National Household Survey of Incidence and Episode Characteristics' (1991) 53 *Journal of Marriage and Family* 805, cited in Beaumont & McEleavy (n 2) 8–9.

[8] A Dyer, 'Report on International Child Abduction by one Parent ("Legal Kidnapping")' Prel. Doc. No 1/1978 [Dyer Report] in *Actes et documents* 1982 (n 6) [21].

[9] Conclusions of the Special Commission of March 1979 on legal kidnapping, in *Actes et documents* 1982 (n 6) [165].

[10] ISS Report (n 6) [138].

[11] United Kingdom Parliament, Hansard (H.C.), vol 946, col 1846, cited in Anton 1981 (n 4) 538.

[12] E Pérez-Vera, 'Explanatory Report' in *Actes et documents* 1982 [Explanatory Report] [34].

Against this backdrop the return mechanism entailed four practical outcomes. Firstly, it succeeded in upholding the primacy of the jurisdiction with which the child had the strongest connection, his habitual residence. Secondly, it prevented the abductor gaining any jurisdictional benefit on the basis of a wrongful act. Thirdly, it usually entailed the child's return to his primary carer for the duration of any subsequent litigation. Finally, it was likely that following this litigation the child would remain in the State of habitual residence with his primary carer, perhaps with some defined travel to the other State to visit his other parent.

The demographic of child abduction has, however, undergone a well-documented paradigm shift, such that the majority of abductors are now primary carer mothers.[13] Consequently, the practical outworking of the return mechanism in many cases leads to a different result from that which was envisaged by the drafters. Return still succeeds in upholding the primacy of the jurisdiction of habitual residence and ensures the abductor gains no advantage by forum shopping. However, return to the State of habitual residence can no longer be equated with effective return to the primary carer for the duration of subsequent litigation. Rather it may entail separation from the primary carer, which can raise important welfare concerns. Additionally, following litigation in that State the original abductor may be allowed to legally relocate with the child, subjecting the child to the disruption of three relocations.

The second view that abduction was contrary to children's interests and welfare led the drafters to craft an instrument which would protect children from the 'harmful effects' of abduction.[14] This view prevailed despite the fact that 'no confirmation could be found for the hypothesis that kidnapping is *always* bad for *a child*'.[15] Rather the framers sought to protect the collective interests of children by deterring abduction. Since the Convention was drafted the concept of children's rights and interests has evolved such that emphasis is now firmly placed on 'the child' as an individual, rather than on 'children' as a notional group. As a result, some have questioned whether the Convention's emphasis on protecting and upholding the interests of children generally pays sufficient regard to the individual interests of the particular child in the particular case.[16]

The difference in the practical outworking of the Convention in what has become the 'typical' case of abduction and the development of the concept of the rights and interests of the child underlie concerns regarding the operation of the instrument. It is submitted that five main concerns primarily and rightly influ-

[13] In 2003 68 per cent of abductors were mothers, 84 per cent of whom were the primary carer, N Lowe, 'A Statistical Analysis of Applications made in 2003 under the Hague Convention of 25 October 1980 on the Civil Aspects of International Child Abduction: Part I: Overall Report' Prel. Doc. No 3/2006 (2007 update) http://hcch.e-vision.nl/upload/wop/abd_pd03e1_2007.pdf 2008 [2003 Study] 21, 23.

[14] Convention on the Civil Aspects of International Child Abduction (adopted 25 October 1980, entered into force 1 December 1983) 1343 UNTS 89, Preamble.

[15] ISS Report (n 6) [138] (first emphasis in original, second emphasis mine).

[16] M Freeman, 'In the Best Interests of Internationally Abducted Children? Plural, Singular, Neither' (2002) *International Family Law* 77 [Freeman 2002]; A Bucher, 'The New Swiss Federal Act on International Child Abduction' (2008) 4 *Journal of Private International Law* 139 [Bucher 2008] 16.

ence current debate: (1) the disruption and trauma created by returning a child only for subsequent litigation in the State of habitual residence to allow the abducting parent to relocate, possibly after several months or even years of 'living in limbo'; (2) the lack of an international regime to promote contact between children and parents living in different States, which can lead to an abusive use of the Convention in inappropriate cases; (3) the welfare of the child and the abducting parent on return to the State of habitual residence, particularly where issues of family violence have been raised; (4) whether the current regime pays sufficient regard to the rights and interests of the individual child; and (5) delays in dealing with applications, and in enforcing return orders, which can cause further harm to the child.

B. Avoiding Multiple Relocations and Promoting Contact

The first and second concerns outlined above are evidenced in the now typical scenario where the primary carer mother abducts the child and the left-behind father either does not want, or is unlikely to be granted, primary care of the child.[17] In these cases:

> There are strong incentives for the parents to find an agreed outcome. For a left behind parent who does not want primary care of the child, there is the prospect of a secure agreed visitation regime. For the taking parent there is the possibility that what originally was a unilateral and unwise act may be re-characterised as an agreed relocation. Most importantly, there is the prospect of limiting damage to the child by avoiding continuing conflict and a situation in which the child may become a shuttlecock between the two countries concerned.[18]

A left-behind parent might seek return, due to the 'often justified fear . . . of losing contact' with the child.[19] However, following litigation in the home State the primary carer and child may be allowed to legally relocate causing the left-behind parent to suffer further distress when the child leaves a second time, and thereby increasing parental conflict:

> The frequent result, following further dislocation, expense, heartache and litigation, is that the children and the primary carer, who originally abducted, are able, legally, to leave the country of habitual residence. However the very process of highly charged litigation and a physical return will often put paid to any prospect of an amicable resolution of the issues. At the same time the children concerned may suffer the trauma of at least three relocations in a short time.[20]

[17] reunite, 'Mediation in International Parental Child Abduction: The reunite Mediation Pilot Scheme' (October 2006) www.reunite.org/edit/files/Mediation%20Report.pdf [reunite Report] 46; in 2003 3 per cent of return applications resulted in access being ordered (26 applications) or agreed (12 applications), 2003 Study (n 13) 30.

[18] reunite Report (n 17) 3 per W Duncan, Deputy Secretary General, Hague Conference.

[19] Questionnaire Responses (ch 1, n 24) Judge Carl.

[20] reunite Report (n 17) 5.

Convention mediation which takes place against the backdrop of both the return mechanism and the subsequent litigation allows the parents to consider the best ultimate option for the child. In this typical scenario the parents might agree to the child remaining in the State of refuge thus avoiding multiple relocations, and mediation can focus on contact arrangements. It is suggested that it is in these cases that mediation can add most value.

C. Welfare Concerns

The Convention seeks to protect the interests of children in three ways: Firstly, in a general sense by creating a deterrent against abduction; secondly, in a specific sense by returning the child to the State with which he has the closest connection; and thirdly, by allowing exceptions to return to protect the specific child where necessary. In this regard the Explanatory Report notes in relation to Article 13(1)(b) that:

> the interest of the child in not being removed from [his] habitual residence without sufficient guarantees of [his] stability in the new environment, gives way before the primary interest of any person in not being exposed to physical or psychological danger or being placed in an intolerable situation.[21]

Authorities dealing with Convention applications are expected to strike the right balance between protecting the child's interests by ordering his return; and protecting his interests by not ordering his return if there is a 'grave risk' that to do so would 'expose the child to physical or psychological harm or otherwise place the child in an intolerable situation'.[22] Convention exceptions are to be 'interpreted in a restrictive fashion' in order not to deprive the instrument of the 'spirit of mutual confidence which is its inspiration'.[23] On this basis judges are wary of usurping the role of their colleagues in the other State and practice in many Contracting States has developed whereby return is only refused where it is considered that the authorities in the State of habitual residence are unable or unwilling to afford appropriate protection following return:

> in most instances where the best interests of the child are paramount in the country of habitual residence the courts of that country will be able to deal with any possible risk to the child, thus overcoming the possible defence of the abducting parent.[24]

While such a construction is generally accepted and further enhanced by the Brussels II *bis* Regulation in the intra-Union context,[25] it is not without its difficulties. The preponderance of abductions by primary carer mothers means that

[21] (n 12) [29].

[22] Art 13(1)(b).

[23] Explanatory Report (n 12) [34].

[24] *A v A* [1996] 2 NZLR 517 cited in P Boshier, 'Care and Protection of Children: New Zealand and Australian Experience of Cross-Border Co-operation' ('4th World Congress on Family Law and Children's Rights', Cape Town, South Africa, March 2005) [Boshier 2005].

[25] Council Regulation (EC) 2201/2003 of 27 November 2003 concerning jurisdiction and the recognition and enforcement of judgments in matrimonial matters and the matters of parental responsibility, repealing Regulation (EC) No 1347/2000 [2003] OJ 338/2 [Brussels II*bis* Regulation], Art 11(4).

return to the State of habitual residence may not equate with a restoration of the *status quo* as intended by the drafters.[26] Rather, return can lead to separation from the primary carer, which is in fact contrary to the original presumption that abduction causes the child to suffer 'the traumatic loss of contact with the parent who has been in charge of his upbringing'.[27]

Judges concerned about welfare issues on return to the State of refuge have been inventive in using mechanisms which uphold the return of the child whilst also seeking to ensure his protection. Judicial networks and liaison judges have been established to facilitate direct communications between judges in different jurisdictions.[28] Additionally, practice has arisen in some States of making a return order subject to undertakings and/or conditions.[29] Such conditions should be of short duration merely to allow safe return and the court 'must be careful not in any way to usurp or be thought to usurp the functions of the court of habitual residence'.[30] Indeed, it has been stated that 'particular care must be exercised to ensure that the competence of the [court in the other State] is not questioned'.[31] Undertakings should 'regulate affairs relating to the children up to but not beyond the door of the court of the children's habitual residence.'[32] They should thus be designed to:

> smooth the return of and to protect the child for the limited period before the foreign court takes over, but they must not be used by the parties to try to clog or fetter, or, in any particular, to delay the enforcement of a paramount decision to return the child.[33]

The use of undertakings has been criticised as putting too much reliance on information received from authorities in other States, the reliability of which cannot easily be ascertained.[34] Additionally, the use of undertakings, though well known in common law States, remains novel in many civil law States.[35] Undertakings are essentially unenforceable promises and although a party may be

[26] Explanatory Report (n 12) [16].

[27] Dyer Report (n 8) [21].

[28] For discussion see P Lortie, 'Report on Judicial Communications in relation to International Child Protection' Prel. Doc. No 8/2006 www.hcch.net/index_en.php?act=publications.details&pid=3893&dtid=2; 'Conclusions and Recommendations of the joint Hague Conference and European Community Conference on Direct Judicial Communications on Family Law Matters and the Development of Judicial Network' (Brussels, Belgium, 15–16 January 2009) www.hcch.net/upload/judcomm_concl2009e.pdf.

[29] 67 cases from 14 jurisdictions on the INCADAT database of Convention cases are listed under the search heading 'undertakings' www.incadat.com.

[30] *Re M (Abduction: Undertakings)* [1995] 1 FLR 1021 [*Re M* [1995]] per Butler-Sloss LJ 1025.

[31] *KS v LS* [2003] NZFLR 817.

[32] *Re M and J (Abduction) (International Judicial Collaboration)* [2000] 1 FLR 803 per Singer J 808–9.

[33] *Re M* [1995] (n 30) 1025.

[34] *D v G* [2001] 1179 HKCU 1.

[35] 'Report on the Fifth Meeting of the Special Commission to Review the Operation of the Hague Convention of 25 October 1980 on the Civil Aspects of International Child Abduction and the Practical Implementation of the Hague Convention of 19 October 1996 on Jurisdiction, Applicable Law, Recognition, Enforcement and Co-Operation in respect of Parental Responsibility and Measures for the Protection of Children' (October–November 2006) Prel. Doc. No 19/2007 http://hcch.e-vision.nl/upload/wop/genaff_pd19e2007.pdf [2006 Report] [227].

required to have these measures registered or 'mirrored' in the other State, in some cases return has been predicated upon a very significant number of undertakings and it seems ambitious to assume that they will necessarily be adhered to.[36] A study found that in two-thirds of cases where undertakings were given they were not kept.[37] This must be a major concern if these undertakings were considered necessary to ensure the safety of the child and the abductor.

The 2006 Special Commission drew up an appendix attached to the Conclusions concerning 'additional considerations relevant to the safe return of the child'.[38] The first point which it was felt the provisions of the Convention supported where appropriate in a particular case was to 'attempt by mediation or conciliation to obtain the voluntary return of the child or the amicable resolution of the issues, in a manner that does not delay the return of the child'.[39] Thus there was agreement that mediation might be a means of addressing some concerns relevant to the safe return of the child. However, there was no further comment as to how this might be done or what safeguards would be required. At the outset it must be recognised that these are often very difficult cases and care needs to be taken to ensure that the mediation process can adequately and safely address these concerns.

Concerns surrounding return include but are not limited to: (1) financial issues—that the abductor neither has resources to accommodate nor provide for everyday needs during subsequent litigation, including retaining a lawyer; (2) criminal issues—that on return the abductor may face criminal sanctions including imprisonment which would enforce separation from the child; (3) emotional issues—that the abductor has no emotional support in the State of habitual residence and may not be able to access the legal system owing to language limitations; and (4) safety issues—that the abductor alleges domestic violence and believes that the State of habitual residence is not able to offer adequate protection.

Some concerns might be adequately addressed in mediation, such as some financial and emotional issues which often lie within the competence of the parents themselves to resolve. For example, a parent may be willing to agree to provide accommodation or financial support to enable the other parent to pursue a legal remedy in the home State. Equally, it may be open to the left-behind parent to drop any criminal charges, and where this is agreed the parties' lawyers could be asked to ensure that these charges have been dropped before the abductor

[36] 'The Permanent Bureau underlined that it was common for the parent giving undertakings to ignore them once the child was returned', ibid.

[37] reunite Research Unit, 'The Outcomes for Children Returned Following an Abduction' September 2003 [31] www.reunite.org/edit/files/Outcomes%20Report.pdf.

[38] 'Conclusions and Recommendations of the Fifth Meeting of the Special Commission to Review the Operation of the Hague Convention of 25 October 1980 on the Civil Aspects of International Child Abduction and the Practical Implementation of the Hague Convention of 19 October 1996 on Jurisdiction, Applicable Law, Recognition, Enforcement and Co-operation in respect of Parental Responsibility and Measures for the Protection of Children (October–November 2006) www.hcch.net/upload/concl28sc5_e.pdf [2006 Conclusions] [16].

[39] ibid. It has been stated that a discussion of mediating conditions for return 'would be insightful and very productive', Questionnaire Responses (ch 1, n 24) Judge Boshier.

returns. Conversely, criminal issues may fall within the remit of the State and thus outside the scope of mediation.

Safety concerns are very often raised in abduction cases[40] and whether mediation can add value in these cases is contentious. In some contexts allegations of domestic violence are a bar to mediation.[41] Proponents of this view highlight the imbalance in the relative negotiating power of the parties which makes it difficult to ensure that agreement was not reached as a result of coercion or fear; and the fact that bringing parties together to mediate can place the alleged victim in danger. Others argue that provided the alleged victim feels safe and is willing to mediate they should be able to. Supporters of this view believe that providing a safe forum in which to discuss the future arrangements for the child can empower the abused, and that concerns can be dealt with through appropriate safeguards.[42]

Such safeguards include primarily the intake session where mediators should be required to screen for domestic violence. Mediators should also be trained to manage the process should abuse be alleged, yet the parties are willing to mediate. Additionally, mediators should work within a domestic violence policy. Ultimately the mediator must be in agreement for mediation to proceed and where it appears that imbalances cannot be addressed or parties cannot be kept safe the mediator should refuse mediation. Where mediation is considered suitable, safeguards must be put in place such as keeping the parties apart both before and after mediation sessions so that they only meet when the mediator is present. If necessary the mediation sessions can proceed by means of a shuttle arrangement whereby parties are situated in different rooms and the mediator moves back and forward between them. The use of distance telecommunications could also offer advantages in these cases.

It is submitted that allegations of domestic violence should not be an absolute bar to mediation. It should be remembered that the alternative is for the alleged victim to defend a Convention court case. The reunite scheme allowed mediation where domestic violence was alleged and the majority of mediators stated that mediation was not hindered despite these allegations.[43] One of the key conclusions of the project was that:

[40] See J Alanen, 'When Human Rights Conflict: Mediating International Parental Kidnapping Disputes Involving the Domestic Violence Defense' (2008) 40 *University of Miami Inter-American Law Review* 49; M Weiner, 'International Child Abduction and the Escape from Domestic Violence' (2000) 69 *Fordham Law Review* 593; M Weiner, 'Symposium: The Potential and Challenges of Transnational Litigation for Feminists concerned about Domestic Violence Here and Abroad' (2003) 11 *American University Journal of Gender Society Policy and Law* 749.

[41] eg legislation in Spain prohibits mediation in cases of domestic violence, *Ley 1/2004 de Medidas de Protección Integral contra la Violencia de Género* Art 44, 'Collated Responses to the Questionnaire concerning the Practical Operation of the Hague Convention of 25 October 1980 on the Civil Aspects of International Child Abduction' Prel. Doc. No 2/2006 http://hcch.e-vision.nl/upload/wop/abd_pd02efs2006.pdf [2006 Responses] 276.

[42] L Parkinson, *Family Mediation* (London, Sweet & Maxwell, 1997) [Parkinson 1997] ch 11; reunite Report (n 17) 48.

[43] reunite Report (n 17) 48.

> Allegations of domestic violence do not preclude entering the mediation process and do not affect the ability to reach a Memorandum of Understanding. However, it is important that a risk assessment is undertaken on each case and appropriate measures introduced to ensure that parents feel safe during the mediation process.[44]

Where issues surrounding the safe return of the child are discussed in mediation and the parents agree on return with various conditions, the Convention application can be dismissed and the court can draw up an enforceable order on the basis of the agreement.[45] Where an agreement seeks to alleviate welfare concerns the parties' legal representatives must ensure that the conditions agreed to are practicable and are capable of ensuring protection. The abducting parent should be advised to seek advanced recognition of the order or mirroring in the other State.[46] Even where the order in principle is automatically enforceable in the other State there is benefit to ensuring that there are no grounds for non-recognition. In this regard Central Authorities and lawyers should be able to offer assistance. The primary advantage of mediation in these cases is that the parties therefore have an enforceable order which deals prima facie with the issues of concern. Conversely, had parties pursued their dispute in the Convention court hearing many of the relevant issues would fall outside the scope of a Convention return order, and would therefore require to be attached as unenforceable undertakings or conditions.

D. The Rights and Interests of the Child

Unless an exception to return is made out, the child will be returned on the basis of a general assumption that return is in the interests of children. Mediation, however, gives the parents the opportunity to reach a solution in the interests of their particular child, without prejudice to the fact that children generally have an interest in being returned. Mediation also allows discussion on broader relevant issues such as contact arrangements which, if resolution is reached, supports the child's right to contact with both parents.[47] Indeed, there is evidence that continuity of contact between a child and his non-resident parent is enhanced when parents formulate agreed solutions. A longitudinal study found that 12 years after their initial dispute resolution:

> [i]n comparison with families who litigated custody, non-residential parents who mediated were more involved in multiple areas of their children's lives, maintained more contact with their children, and had a greater influence in co-parenting.[48]

[44] ibid 53.

[45] See ch 3, III.H.

[46] Convention on Jurisdiction, Applicable Law, Recognition, Enforcement and Co-operation in respect of Parental Responsibility and Measures for the Protection of Children (adopted 19 October 1996, entered into force 1 January 2002) 35 ILM 1391 [1996 Hague Convention] Art 23.

[47] Convention on the Rights of the Child (adopted 20 November 1989, entered into force 2 September 1990) 1577 UNTS 3 [United Nations Convention] Arts 9(3) and 10(2).

[48] R Emery et al, 'Child Custody Mediation and Litigation: Custody, Contact and Coparenting 12 Years after Initial Dispute Resolution' (2001) 69 *Journal of Consulting and Clinical Psychology* 323 [Emery 2001].

This study followed American families over a 12-year period and it is too early to say whether Convention mediation will improve the continuity of relationship between a child and a non-resident parent given the fact that the child and parent now reside in different States. However, granting parents the opportunity to negotiate pertinent issues in the best interests of their particular child or children certainly goes some way to addressing concerns that the Convention proceedings do not pay sufficient regard to the interests of the individual child.

On the other hand, while focusing on the specific circumstances of the particular dispute automatically puts the interests of the individual child to the fore, mediation does not guarantee respect for those interests. While it is to be hoped that parents ultimately seek solutions which benefit their children, it is not always easy in the midst of conflict for a parent to separate the child's interest from his own interests and 'there is no guarantee that all parents will make a decision concerning their children primarily on the basis of the children's welfare.'[49] However, an important difference between domestic mediation and Convention mediation is that in the latter the authorities of the States have been seised by the Convention application which to an extent puts the dispute into the public realm. There is therefore justification for insisting that certain rights are taken account of in a way not deemed necessary in domestic family mediation. This issue is discussed in more detail in chapter five in the specific context of the child's right to be heard. Additionally, in the Convention context parties should be encouraged to have their agreement drawn up as an enforceable order, which also gives the court the opportunity to ensure the interests of the child have been sufficiently taken into account. Failure to have done so could be grounds for non-enforceability of the agreement.[50]

E. Delays

Mediation can also offer a response to the final concern raised above regarding delays in reaching outcomes and in enforcing return orders. The addition of an extra process into the system for handling a Convention case can of course cause some delay. However, this book has sought to show that by establishing a specialist scheme to fit within the Convention regime, delay can be minimal. Convention mediation can take place expeditiously and therefore need not result in any undue delay.[51] Additionally, owing to the broader scope of mediation the ultimate issue can be resolved in one step, reducing the time taken to reach final outcome. In this regard, it should be remembered that litigation to deal with the merits of the dispute following the Convention decision does not fall within the expeditious

[49] S Minamikata, 'Resolution of Disputes over Parental Rights and Duties in a Marital Dissolution Case in Japan: A Non-litigious Approach in *Chotei* (Family Court Mediation)' [2005–06] 39 *Family Law Quarterly* 489 [Minamikata 2006] 506.

[50] See ch 3, III.H and ch 5, IV.

[51] ch 3, III.C.

Convention regime, but takes place under normal domestic procedure and can drag on for many months or even years. Secondly, while parties will be encouraged to have their agreement drawn up as a domestic court order so that it is enforceable,[52] negotiated agreements are more likely to be adhered to thus reducing the need for enforcement.[53]

III. Additional Added Value

A. Introduction

In addition to offering a response to current concerns regarding the operation of the instrument mediation offers further added value in the Convention context. Firstly, there are benefits inherent in the process which can improve family relationships. Secondly, developing Convention mediation does not require legislative amendment at the international level and can thus take place expeditiously and relatively easily.

B. Benefits Inherent in the Mediation Process

In the Convention context outcome is particularly important as where parents fail to reach agreement in mediation their dispute will fall to be resolved by the courts. However, mediation is a process and there are benefits inherent in the process regardless of the outcome. As there is so little cross-border family mediation occurring in practice, it is necessary to discuss the benefits of process primarily by extrapolation from research evidence in the domestic context.[54] The Council of Europe Recommendation was premised on the 'results of research into the use of mediation and experiences in this area in several countries',[55] which demonstrated that family mediation had the potential to: (1) improve communication between members of the family; (2) reduce conflict between the parties in dispute; (3) produce amicable settlements; (4) provide continuity of personal contacts between parents and children; (5) reduce social and economic costs for the parties and the State; and (6) reduce the length of time otherwise required to settle the conflict.

[52] ch 3, III.H.

[53] J Kelly, 'Family Mediation Research: Is There Empirical Support for the Field?' (2004) 22 *Conflict Resolution Quarterly* 3 [Kelly 2004] 28.

[54] The author wrote to eminent family mediation researchers to enquire about research in the international context. The replies stated that there was no research of which they were aware, Robert Emery (19 September 2008); Joan Kelly (19 September 2008) and Lisa Parkinson (various). The author is grateful for these responses.

[55] 'Explanatory Memorandum to Recommendation No R(98)1 of the Committee of Ministers to Member States on Family Mediation' [Council of Europe Memorandum] [7].

When family mediation first emerged in the United States it was promoted as being:

> less expensive and time-consuming, more humane and satisfying to participants than litigation, resulting in better compliance with agreements and reduced re-litigation. It was expected to enhance problem-solving skills among the disputants, promote co-operation and communication regarding children, and result in better adjustment of adults and their children . . . and be more empowering of the participants than traditional adversarial processes.[56]

While there was no empirical evidence at the time to back up such sweeping optimism, there was a sense in many States that the courts 'did not always seem very effective in dealing with divorce and related matters in ways that were helpful to the parties or their children'.[57] The adversarial nature of the court process, which effectively establishes a winner and a loser, was not in keeping with the growing understanding of the benefits of maintaining an ongoing relationship between the child and both his parents.[58] Additionally, there was an increased recognition of the importance of 'private ordering'[59] in family disputes which questioned whether the courts, as the coercive judicial power of the State, were the appropriate body to intervene in the private realm of family life.[60] Against this backdrop mediation was viewed by many as a means of modernising the family justice system.

Research has subsequently found that parents: 'who use custody mediation are substantially more satisfied than parents using other court processes'.[61] There is greater adherence to agreements which are generally more durable,[62] and mediation can reduce conflict and improve communication, promoting continuing agreement as opposed to litigation which can be conflict enhancing.[63] In this regard it has been described as the 'paradox of family mediation'[64] that more is asked of parents when they are in dispute than when they are not. 'There are

[56] Kelly 2004 (n 53) 3.

[57] D Macfarlane, 'Family Mediation in France' (2004) 10 *Journal of Family Studies* 97 [Macfarlane 2004].

[58] United Nations Convention (n 47) Arts 9(3) and 10(2).

[59] See s 1(5) of the Children Act 1989 in England and Wales as an example of this preference for 'private ordering'. This section states that: 'Where a court is considering whether or not to make one or more orders under this Act with respect to a child, it shall not make the order or any of the orders unless it considers that doing so would be better for the child than making no order at all'.

[60] S Cretney, 'Conciliation, Reconciliation and Mediation in the Historical Context' in J Westcott (ed), *Family Mediation – Past, Present and Future* (Bristol, Family Law, 2004).

[61] Kelly 2004 (n 53) 29.

[62] A study found a 50–75 per cent reduction in custody hearings when parents participated in court-based mediation programmes, cited in J Zawid, 'Practical and Ethical Implications of Mediating International Child Abduction Cases: A New Frontier for Mediators' (2008) 40 *University of Miami Inter-American Law Review* 1 [Zawid 2008] fn 36; Kelly 2004 (n 53) 28; Emery 2001 (n 48) 323; J Hunt and C Roberts, 'Intervening in Litigated Contact: Ideas from other Jurisdictions' 2005, cited in National Audit Office, 'Legal Services Commission: Legal Aid and Mediation for People Involved in Family Breakdown' HC 256 Session 2006–07 (March 2007) www.nao.org.uk [Legal Services Commission Report] 26.

[63] Council of Europe Memorandum (n 55) [7].

[64] Parkinson 1997 (n 42) ch 2.

expectations of reasonableness, at a time when reason may be swamped by anger and misery'.[65] Encouraging and assisting parents to communicate directly, rather than through lawyers, creates the basis for improving communication. Additionally, assisting parents to negotiate and compromise rather than argue a position can reduce conflict. A study comparing parents who litigated and parents who mediated found that the latter, 'made more changes in their children's living arrangements over the years. For the most part, the changes apparently reflect increased co-operation and flexibility'.[66] Additionally, it was shown that the 'increased involvement of non-residential parents . . . did not lead to an associated increase in co-parenting conflict'.[67]

84 per cent of participants in the reunite scheme stated that mediation was 'helpful' or 'very helpful' in improving communication, with the majority of these finding it very helpful.[68] Similarly, 83 per cent of participants stated that mediation was 'helpful' or 'very helpful' in reducing conflict.[69] Convention cases are often highly conflicted as any existing conflict is likely to have been exacerbated by the abduction. However, '[m]ediation has given evidence of its power to settle complex, highly emotional disputes'.[70] Part of the role of a mediator is to diffuse conflict in order to enable the parties to focus on the best interests of their child. Importantly, where conflict can be reduced there is generally a greater likelihood of ongoing contact between the child and the non-resident parent without the need for future court intervention. Indeed, 'co-operation and agreement in one area can help to maintain trust and increase co-operation in other areas'.[71] Where parents will be living in different States the ability to communicate to resolve future disputes without the need for potentially costly cross-border litigation has obvious advantages. In this regard abducted children tend to be relatively young[72] and thus the ongoing interaction of the parents may be necessary for many years. Assisting parents to improve communication and reduce conflict promotes party autonomy not just for the present dispute but also in the future interests of the parties and their children.

C. Wider Added Value

Convention mediation can add value in at least two other regards. Firstly, it is a means through which Contracting States can continue to improve the implementation and operation of the Convention without the need for legislative amendment,

[65] ibid.
[66] Emery 2001 (n 48) 323.
[67] ibid.
[68] Only 11 per cent categorised it as 'not helpful' and only five per cent as 'unhelpful', reunite Report (n 17) 24.
[69] Only 17 per cent found it 'not helpful' or 'unhelpful', ibid 23.
[70] Kelly 2004 (n 53) 28.
[71] Parkinson 1997 (n 42) ch 2.
[72] 2003 Study (n 13) 27–8.

at least at the international level.[73] Some further structures may be required at a domestic level to support the mediation process, for example with regard to the training and qualification of mediators. However, in general mediation can be introduced on the basis of co-operative non-legislative measures.[74] By contrast, there have been suggestions over the last decade that in the light of some of the concerns regarding the operation of the Convention, it should be amended by means of a Protocol.[75] A specific proposal was put to the 2006 Special Commission[76] which recognised the 'potential value of a Protocol' but did not consider it 'an immediate priority'.[77] Without prejudice to discussions on the utility of a Protocol, and regardless of whether or not aspects of the use of mediation could later become enshrined in any Protocol (which could be very useful), the development of Convention mediation can proceed irrespective of such discussions. Mediation can thus be implemented relatively quickly and on a State-by-State basis without the need for the consensus that would be required for the introduction of a Protocol.

Secondly, structures developed in the context of mediating return applications under the Convention may be adaptable for use in Convention applications concerning contact,[78] and abduction cases which fall outside the Convention regime.[79] The effective protection of contact between a child and a non-resident parent remains a gap in the international regime despite the enactment of various instruments.[80] Convention mediation can offer a limited response in those cases where

[73] See Guide to Good Practice: *Part II on Implementing Measures* (Bristol, Family Law, 2003) [Guide on Implementing Measures] 20–1.

[74] In the Convention context much has been achieved by adapting and improving practice, without the need for legislative amendment. The Permanent Bureau provides a number of invaluable 'post-Convention services' well documented and accessible on the Hague Conference website www.hcch.net/index_en.php?act=text.display&tid=21. Central Authority personnel, lawyers and judges have also worked tirelessly to improve the operation of the Convention and experts' meetings and academic debate have also contributed to the successful working of the instrument.

[75] 'Conclusions of the Special Commission of May 2000 on General Affairs and Policy of the Conference' Prel. Doc. No 10/2000 www.hcch.net/upload/wop/genaff2000concl_e.pdf.

[76] See 2006 Report (n 35) [251–4].

[77] 2006 Conclusions (n 38) [1.8.3].

[78] Reference is made to two cross-border contact cases which were mediated in Quebec, Canada. With the agreement of both parents and both Central Authorities mediation in each case was undertaken over a few months and resulted in an agreement, Questionnaire Responses (ch 1, n 24) Lorraine Filion.

[79] In this regard important work is being done under the auspices of the Hague Conference, between certain Contracting States and certain non-Contracting States of an Islamic tradition in the context of the 'Malta Process'. The States support the development of mediation structures to handle abduction cases arising between these States, Third Malta Judicial Conference on Cross-Frontier Family Law Issues, hosted by the Government of Malta in collaboration with the Hague Conference on Private International Law www.hcch.net/upload/maltadecl09_e.pdf, reunite has also established mediation in abduction cases concerning Egypt, information from Denise Carter.

[80] The 1996 Hague Convention (n 46) will add value when ratified on a broader scale. See also Convention on Contact Concerning Children (adopted 15 May 2003, entered into force 1 September 2005) ETS No 192; W Duncan, 'Transfrontier Access/Contact General Principles and Good Practice' Prel. Doc. No 4/2006 http://hcch.e-vision.nl/upload/wop/abd_pd04e2006.pdf; *General Principles and Guide to Good Practice on Transfrontier Contact Concerning Children* (Bristol, Family Law, 2008).

an application is made for return but where the primary focus is in fact contact.[81] However, the availability of Convention mediation should not encourage applications for return in order that a party can utilise the advantageous Convention mediation process as a means of securing contact and Convention professionals should be watchful to ensure that this does not become the practice.

Certainly, Convention mediation is not a solution to either the absence of a regime to support cross-border contact, or the absence of a regime for non-Convention abductions. However, the existence of a functioning mediation system for Convention cases and experienced and trained mediators could offer a useful first step. It is suggested that the development of mediation in both these areas requires further discussion primarily owing to the absence of an adequate legal framework. It is therefore important to emphasise that the development of Convention mediation will not only support return applications arising under the instrument but could also act as a catalyst for the development of cross-border family mediation in other contexts, where it may be a particular advantage. In this regard the Hague Conference has established a Working Party on mediation in the context of its work with States not yet party to the Convention, primarily States with an Islamic culture.[82]

IV. Conclusion

This chapter addressed the question 'why offer mediation in Convention cases?' with a view to not only validating the current enthusiasm but moving that enthusiasm into action by highlighting the added value offered by mediation. Firstly, mediation can offer a response to some of the concerns regarding the operation of the Convention in the present day. Secondly, the mediation process enhances relationships and encourages private ordering and party autonomy which offers value for the family in the present and also into the future. Thirdly, mediation can proceed without the need for legislative amendment. Fourthly, establishing Convention mediation could act as a catalyst for the development of cross-border mediation in other areas. The added value thus justifies the resources necessary to develop Convention mediation notwithstanding the legal remedy already offered by the instrument.

[81] There is certainly anecdotal evidence that 'in some cases parents had applied for a return when really they would be happy with contact' reunite Report (n 17) 46.

[82] See ch 1, n 18.

5

The Voice of the Child

I. Introduction

The previous chapters sought to give a general overview of Convention mediation. These chapters intentionally addressed the issues broadly given the newness of the discipline and the range of matters that require further discussion at this early stage of development. The present chapter focuses in more detail upon one specific issue which is particularly topical and important, yet has not been discussed in detail elsewhere: the voice of the child. This issue sits at the cusp of two current debates, one regarding whether and how to hear a child in domestic family mediation; and the other regarding whether and how to hear a child in Convention court proceedings. This chapter outlines not only how the voice of the child can be heard in Convention mediation, but also suggests that the views of the child can be better taken into account through mediation, offering a concrete and important example of the added value of Convention mediation.

II. The Voice of the Child in Mediation

The predominant mediation model in most States is 'child-focused' whereby the child is usually not heard. There are mechanisms to enable the child to be heard, either by the mediator or another professional, and for his views to be fed-back to his parents in mediation, but this is not the norm and in reality children are 'not often directly involved'.[1] 'Child-inclusive' mediation by contrast actively promotes and encourages hearing the child. The mechanisms are generally the same with the child being heard separately by a mediator or other professional and his views fed-back to his parents. The difference between the two models 'is not so much a change of policy, more a change of emphasis'.[2]

[1] International Social Service Family Mediation Trainers Group (Geneva 2005) in L Parkinson, 'Cross-Border Family Mediation: Opportunities, Difficulties and Experience' (ERA Conference on Cross-Border Family Mediation, Trier, Germany, April 2007) [Parkinson 2007].

[2] Mediation in Divorce 'Listening to Young People' 2004, cited in L Parkinson, 'Child-inclusive Family Mediation' (2006) *Family Law* 483 [Parkinson 2006] 485.

There is no requirement to hear a child in mediation. A presumption in law that a child should be heard[3] does not extend to mediation and does not intend to impinge upon the private realm of the family.[4] Indeed, in mediation protection of the rights and interests of the child stays within the remit of the parents, unless child protection concerns are raised. Parents are not bound to respect their child's right to be heard, and indeed it may seem incongruous with the promotion of party autonomy and private ordering to require, or operate a presumption, that the child's voice should be heard. To do so leads to concern that hearing the child 'undermines the parents' control over their decisions – one of the main tenets of mediation'.[5]

While these are essentially arguments concerned with preserving the parents' autonomy, there are also child-centric reasons why hearing a child might be inappropriate. The child's absence is often seen as a means of actually protecting his rights and interests. It is recognised that hearing a child can place him in a position of particular vulnerability as 'children are dependent upon their parents, and if their points of view are in conflict with those of their parents, this may be harmful to the child'.[6] Difficulties may be created in the parent-child relationship where views are expressed but not reflected in the subsequent parental agreement. These reasons have led to concern that owing to the familial nature of the dispute, hearing a child in mediation, 'increase[s] conflicts of loyalty for children and burden[s] them with choices and inappropriate responsibility' additionally it might 'cause repercussions for the child including rejection and punishment'.[7] Alternatively there is concern that parents may pay too much attention to the views of the child and that this 'gives a child too much power to influence or even decide outcome'.[8] It is consequently often with a view to protecting both the rights of the parents and the interests of the child that mediators prefer a child-focused approach.

However, there are also other less cogent reasons why children are rarely heard in mediation. Generally parental permission is required unlike in court proceedings where the child's right to express his views persists independently of his parents' wishes either presumptively or on his own request.[9] It is partly because the parents are essentially the gatekeepers to their children's views that even where child-inclusive mediation is encouraged, take up is low. '[I]f the child's view is unlikely to coincide with one parent's view, that parent is unlikely to want the child's view to be heard'.[10] As a result a mediation provider which moved to a

[3] Convention on the Rights of the Child (adopted 20 November 1989, entered into force 2 September 1990) 1577 UNTS 3 [United Nations Convention] Art 12.

[4] ibid Art 5.

[5] Parkinson 2006 (n 2) 484.

[6] K Skjørten and R Barlindhaug, 'The Involvement of Children in Decisions about Shared Residence' (2007) 21 *International Journal of Law Policy and the Family* 373, 374.

[7] Parkinson 2007 (n 1).

[8] ibid.

[9] 'Collated Responses to the Questionnaire concerning the Practical Operation of the Hague Convention of 25 October 1980 on the Civil Aspects of International Child Abduction' Prel. Doc. No 2/2006 http://hcch.e-vision.nl/upload/wop/abd_pd02efs2006.pdf [2006 Responses] 107–26.

[10] Parkinson 2006 (n 2) 484.

child-inclusive model noted that '[e]ven with a policy to encourage children's involvement, they are actually involved in only a minority of cases'.[11]

Another anomaly raised by the fact that the parents are the decision-makers in mediation is that they do not have the same access to the child's expressed views as a judge would have in court proceedings. Any views expressed by a child in mediation are usually subject to the same degree of confidentiality afforded to the parents' negotiations. That is that with the exception of any child protection concern, anything a child says is confidential. In this respect a child chooses which if any of his views expressed to a mediator are reported back to his parents. Therefore the parents will not necessarily have full access to the expressed views of the child, unlike the judge.

A certain amount of preparatory work is necessary in order that the parents and the child are aware of the confidential nature of hearing a child in mediation. By way of example practice in Scotland[12] involves the mediator meeting with the parents to discuss the child's participation. The parents will be informed that the child will be invited to express views but will not be asked to make decisions; and that the child will choose which views to feed-back to the parents. Parents are encouraged not to ask their child to tell them what they have said to the mediator but to wait for the appointed feedback session. An important element of this meeting with the parents is to prepare them for the fact that they might hear information that they do not wish to hear and that they should not agree to the child being heard unless they are able to acknowledge this. If the mediator is satisfied that it would not cause harm to the child a letter is sent to the child inviting him to come and speak with a mediator. At this meeting the mediator explains the confidentiality rules to the child and seeks his views. Older children are invited to report their own views back to their parents; however, they rarely accept this offer and usually prefer the mediator to relay the relevant information.[13]

In light of the cautions raised above it is not surprising that hearing a child in mediation remains unusual.[14] However, it has been suggested that absenting children from the process as a means of protecting them may be overly paternalistic and that children can cope with and indeed desire to be heard.[15] Given the confidentiality which is attached to the child's views and the fact that views are fed-back to the parents through a mediator, many of the concerns raised above may be overstated. Indeed research into the effects of child-inclusive mediation has shown many positive benefits which are likely to influence future practice.

One of the earliest studies on child-inclusive mediation found that 25 out of 28 children felt 'they had benefited in some way from their attendance . . . most of

[11] ibid 485.

[12] This practice is almost identical to English practice, ibid 485–6.

[13] Given the importance and complexities of listening to a child in mediation, mediators generally require additional training in order to do this work.

[14] J Achim, F Cyr and L Filion, 'L'implication de l'enfant en médiation familiale: de la théorie à la pratique' (1997) 18:1 *Revue québécoise de psychologie* 41, 41.

[15] Children are 'more competent to take part in family decision-making than adults generally consider them to be and less vulnerable than adults fear', Parkinson 2006 (n 2) 488.

them mentioning a definite improvement in communication'.[16] 13 out of 15 parents were also positive about their child's attendance at mediation, the most frequently mentioned benefits being 'improved communication and better access arrangements.'[17] While this research is well known and still discussed in literature, it did not lead to a change in practice. However, 20 years on, against the backdrop of the children's rights movement and the general acceptance that children should be heard in welfare-based court proceedings, research evidence of the positive effects of child-inclusive mediation is likely to have greater impact.

Recent empirical research comparing outcomes for children and families in child-focused and child-inclusive models demonstrates a range of benefits in the latter approach. These include: a clear emphasis on the child's needs; empowerment of the child by increasing his or her knowledge of the situation; improvement of child-parent communication; an increase in the likelihood that children are aware of parental co-operation; an enhancement of an aligned parental view; and significant improvement in the quality of the resultant agreement.[18] The foremost empirical research to date compared outcomes of child-inclusive mediation and child-focused mediation over a one-year period in Australia.[19] The first group evidenced greater relationship improvements and psychological well-being, these effects being strongest for fathers and children. Agreements reached by this group were significantly more durable, parents in the other group being twice as likely to instigate new litigation within a year of mediation.[20]

Evidence of positive benefits for children and their families is bound to lead to further thought on whether children should be heard more frequently in mediation. However, while mediators might move towards encouraging the involvement of children, the ultimate decision rests with the parents.

III. The Voice of the Child in Convention Court Proceedings

The second influential debate concerns the voice of the child in Convention court proceedings. The only reference to the voice of the child in the Convention is Article 13(2) which states that return may be refused if the authorities find that 'the child objects to being returned and has attained an age and degree of maturity

[16] F Garwood, 'Children in Conciliation: The Experience of Involving Children in Conciliation' 28 (1989) *Family and Conciliation Courts Review* 43, 50.

[17] ibid.

[18] Outcomes from an empirical study of 17 families in New Zealand: J Goldson, '*Hello, I'm a Voice, Let Me Talk*: Child-Inclusive Mediation in Family Separation' The Families Commission Innovative Practice Report No 1/06, December 2006, 7.

[19] J McIntosh et al, 'Child-Focused and Child-Inclusive Divorce Mediation: Comparative Outcomes from a Prospective Study of Postseparation Adjustment' (2008) 46 *Family Court Review* 105.

[20] ibid 113–14.

at which it is appropriate to take account of [his] views'. This places three important limits on the child's voice in the Convention case: firstly, the views of the child are only explicitly relevant in so far as he objects to return.[21] Secondly, the child's age and degree of maturity are important in establishing whether to take his views into account.[22] Thirdly, the court retains discretion to order return notwithstanding that an age-appropriate and mature child has expressed a clear objection.[23]

This provision was included given that the Convention applies, *ratione personae*, to all children under the age of 16 and 'it would be very difficult to accept that a child of, for example, fifteen years of age, should be returned against [his] will'.[24] While no minimum age was agreed as all suggestions 'seemed artificial, even arbitrary',[25] the implication seems to be that the provision was intended to apply in the context of older teenagers. An interesting finding of the 1999 and 2003 Studies is that the age range of abducted children remained fairly static. In both years 42 per cent of children were aged five to nine and most other children were younger than five.[26] Teenagers accounted for only 6 per cent of the sample in the 2003 Study.[27] Against this backdrop few abducted children meet the age and maturity requirement as intended by the drafters. While there is no accurate data on how many children objected to return yet were nevertheless ordered returned, there were very few cases in 2003 where the objections of a child were determinative in preventing return.[28]

Historically, Contracting States have taken different approaches to the application of Article 13(2). In some jurisdictions the views of the child, considered to be of appropriate age and maturity, are generally sought in order to determine whether he objects to return.[29] In other jurisdictions the child's views are normally only

[21] It is well established in Convention jurisprudence that the objection must be to returning to the State not the parent.

[22] The framers could not agree on a minimum age so an assessment of appropriate age and maturity is at the discretion of each State, E Pérez-Vera, 'Explanatory Report' in *Actes et documents de la quatorzième session, Tome III, Enlèvement d'enfants* (Hague Conference, The Hague, 1982) 426 [Explanatory Report] [30].

[23] Convention on the Civil Aspects of International Child Abduction (adopted 25 October 1980, entered into force 1 December 1983) 1343 UNTS 89, Arts 13 and 18.

[24] Explanatory Report (n 22) [30].

[25] ibid.

[26] Children aged up to four years constituted 38 per cent of the sample in 1999; and 36 per cent in 2003, N Lowe, 'A Statistical Analysis of Applications made in 2003 under the Hague Convention of 25 October 1980 on the Civil Aspects of International Child Abduction: Part I: Overall Report' Prel. Doc. No 3/2006 (2007 update) http://hcch.e-vision.nl/upload/wop/abd_pd03e1_2007.pdf 2008 [2003 Study] 27–8.

[27] ibid 27. There was no equivalent data in the 1999 Study, N Lowe, S Armstrong and A Mathias, 'A Statistical Analysis of Applications made in 1999 under the Hague Convention of 25 October 1980 on the Civil Aspects of International Child Abduction' Prel. Doc. No 3/2001 (Revised version, November 2001) http://hcch.e-vision.nl/upload/abd2001pd3e.pdf.

[28] 2003 Study (n 26) 37–8. Only 13 per cent of cases ended in judicial refusal. 9 per cent of these were due to the child's objections and in another 12 cases the child's objections were one of the reasons for the refusal. Most children whose objections were decisive were over 11 and the youngest child was eight.

[29] eg in Finland under the Child Custody and Rights of Access Act, Art 39; Germany under the Act on Matters concerned with Non-contentious Litigation (FGG), s 50d; Lithuania under the Civil Code, Art 3.164(1); Poland under the Constitution, Art 72§3; and Romania under Law No 369/2004. Also in

sought where an Article 13(2) exception is raised, usually by the abducting parent.[30] Both approaches are Convention compatible, there being no general obligation to hear a child, and interestingly the different approaches do not appear to affect outcome. While traditionally children are heard far more frequently in for example Germany, as opposed to England and Wales, in 2003 none of the 80 incoming applications to Germany was refused on the basis of the child's objections and the exception was successfully upheld in just two of the 142 incoming applications to England and Wales.[31] While not expressly stated in the Convention, a child's views may also be relevant in establishing other exceptions to return, notably under Article 12(2) and Article 13(1)(b); however, these exceptions were also 'interpreted in a restrictive fashion',[32] as intended by the drafters, in both jurisdictions in 2003.[33]

Although Article 13(2) is the only Convention provision which refers to the voice of the child, the instrument sits within a broader legal framework and must be interpreted in the light of generally agreed principles. Notable in this regard is the United Nations Convention on the Rights of the Child,[34] which is almost universally accepted and therefore bears testimony to consensus in the international community with regard to certain rights and interests of the child.[35] Article 12 states that the child who is capable of forming his own views has a right to express those views freely, and for this purpose to be provided with the opportunity to be heard in any judicial and administrative proceedings affecting him. It is widely accepted that even very young children are capable of forming their own views and therefore this provision has a very broad application. Age and maturity is not a factor in establishing whether a child should be heard but only becomes relevant with regard to how much weight to attach to his views.[36]

Austria, China (Macau Special Administrative Region), Czech Republic, Denmark and The Netherlands, 2006 Responses (n 9) 107–25.

[30] eg in England and Wales see *Re M (A Minor) (Child Abduction)* [1994] 1 FLR 390 per Butler-Sloss LJ 394. For discussion see M Freeman and A Hutchinson, 'The Voice of the Child in International Child Abduction' (2007) *International Family Law* 177 [Freeman & Hutchinson, 2007] and P McEleavy, 'Evaluating the Views of Abducted Children: Trend in Appellate Case-law' (2008) *Child and Family Law Quarterly* 230 [McEleavy 2008]. Also in China (Hong Kong Special Administrative Region) and Cyprus, 2006 Responses (n 9) 107–25.

[31] N Lowe et al, 'A Statistical Analysis of Applications made in 2003 under the Hague Convention of 25 October 1980 on the Civil Aspects of International Child Abduction: Part II: National Reports' Prel. Doc. No 3/2008 (2007 update) http://hcch.evision.nl/upload/wop/abd_pd03ef2007.pdf [2003 Study – National Reports] 221, 463. In 1999, one out of 70 applications to Germany and two out of 149 applications to England and Wales resulted in a refusal based on the child's objections, Germany – National Report http://hcch.e-vision.nl/upload/stats_de.pdf 13; United Kingdom – National Report http://hcch.e-vision.nl/upload/stats_uktot.pdf 14.

[32] Explanatory Report (n 22) [34].

[33] In Germany return was refused in two cases on the basis of Art 13(1)(b). In England and Wales there were no refusals based on either of these grounds, 2003 Study – National Reports (n 31) 221, 463.

[34] United Nations Convention (n 3). The Committee on the Rights of the Child has encouraged States Parties to ratify the Hague Convention as a way of fulfilling their obligations under Art 11 [General Observations No 5 (2003)].

[35] (n 34) only Somalia and the United States have not adhered to this Convention http://treaties.un.org/Pages/ViewDetails.aspx?src=TREATY&mtdsg_no=IV11&chapter=4&lang=en.

[36] Art 12(1).

The seeming disparity between the wording of Article 12 of the United Nations Convention and established practice under the Hague Convention in several States until recently appeared to concern commentators more than the courts.[37] Courts recognise that Convention proceedings are primarily an issue of forum rather than substance. The merits of the case are left to be addressed in subsequent litigation where authorities can conduct a full welfare-based hearing, including, where appropriate, hearing the child. As Convention proceedings are summary in nature courts in many States have been satisfied that there is no requirement to hear a child. The Convention hearing involves the need to balance different and sometimes competing rights and interests and the instrument is considered to be 'broadly compatible'[38] with the United Nations Convention. Adherence to the former is a mechanism through which States can give general effect to their obligations under Article 11 of the latter.[39] Prompt return to the State of habitual residence is generally considered to be in a child's best interests,[40] and can also facilitate in the individual case, contact between a child and a non-resident parent.[41] Thus the rights and interests of the child which are protected by a summary hearing for swift return have tended to triumph over giving the child an opportunity to express his views.

However, the application of the Brussels II *bis* Regulation to intra-European Union cases since March 2005 has altered the legal landscape. The Regulation states that:

> When applying Articles 12 and 13 of the 1980 Hague Convention, it shall be ensured that the child is given the opportunity to be heard during the proceedings unless this appears inappropriate having regard to his or her age or degree of maturity.[42]

Despite the traditional reluctance of the English courts to hear children in Convention cases, it has been acknowledged by the House of Lords that this provision applies 'in any case in which the court is being asked to . . . direct the summary return of the child – in effect in every Hague Convention case'.[43] It 'erects a presumption that the child will be heard unless this appears inappropriate'.[44] It was further stated that the principle is 'of universal application and consistent with our international obligations under Article 12 of the [United Nations

[37] See R Schuz, 'Protection Versus Autonomy: The Child Abduction Experience' in Y Ronen and C Greenbaum, *The Case for the Child: Towards a New Agenda* (Antwerp, Intersentia, 2008) [Schuz 2008]; A Greene, 'Seen and Not Heard?: Children's Objections Under the Hague Convention on International Child Abduction' (2005) 13 *University of Miami International and Comparative Law Review* 105.

[38] N Lowe, M Everall and M Nicholls, *International Movement of Children* (Bristol, Family Law, 2004) [17.156]. See also ch 1, III.

[39] General Observations No 5 (2003), (n 34).

[40] Art 3.

[41] Art 9.

[42] Council Regulation (EC) 2201/2003 of 27 November 2003 concerning jurisdiction and the recognition and enforcement of judgments in matrimonial matters and the matters of parental responsibility, repealing Regulation (EC) No 1347/2000 [2003] OJ 338/2 [Brussels II *bis* Regulation] Art 11(2).

[43] *Re D (A Child) (Abduction: Foreign Custody Rights)* [2006] UKHL 51 per Baroness Hale of Richmond [*Re D* [2006]] 58.

[44] ibid.

Convention]'.[45] As such the impact of this provision is likely to extend beyond intra-Union cases.[46] Recent case law in Ireland shows a similar trend.[47] Outside the European Union there is also some movement towards hearing children more frequently in Convention cases.[48]

Under the Brussels II *bis* Regulation there is no requirement to hear a child if it is 'inappropriate' owing to his age or maturity. The provision is therefore narrower than Article 12 of the United Nations Convention; however, it is in line with most domestic legislation which purportedly seeks to give effect to Article 12. Although practice differs from State to State, the usual age at which a child is required to be heard in domestic family proceedings across the range of Contracting States is 12.[49] Younger than 12 judges generally have a discretion as to whether the child should be heard on the basis that he may be too young or too immature. In the context of the Hague Convention very few abducted children are aged 12 or older.[50] It remains to be seen whether States will be accorded a broad or narrow discretion in interpreting when a child's age and maturity make it 'inappropriate' to hear that child. However, while the Brussels II *bis* Regulation imports an age and maturity gateway, analysis of the early cases seems to indicate that States are interpreting the provision as requiring children even at a very young age to be given the opportunity to express their views.[51] Practice in England and Wales is now that 'all children in Hague Convention cases, except those who

[45] ibid.

[46] At least this is likely to be the case in incoming applications to England and Wales 46 per cent of which involved non-Community States in 2003, 2003 Study (n 26) 449.

[47] *In the Matter of M. N. (A Child)* [2009] IEHC 213 [*M. N.* [2009]]; see also C McGuinness, 'The Voice of the Child in Irish Cases on the Hague Convention on Child Abduction 1980' (International Family Justice Judicial Conference for Common Law and Commonwealth Jurisdictions, Windsor, England, August 2009) [2009 Windsor Conference] [McGuinness 2009]; A Daly, 'Considered or Merely Heard? The Views of Young Children in Hague Convention Cases in Ireland' [2009] 1 *Irish Journal of Family Law* 16 [Daly 2009].

[48] In Israel reg 295(9) of the Civil Procedure Regulations, which applies in Convention cases, grants a child a general right to be heard; however, until recently the 'special reasons' exception contained in this provision was often relied upon and children were not routinely heard. However the Supreme Court in *Request for Family Appeal 5579/07 Plonit v Ploni* tak-al 07(3) 2054 (2007) held that children should normally be heard in Convention cases. See R Schuz, 'The Voice of the Child in the Israeli Family Court' in B Atkin and F Banda, *The International Survey of Family Law* (Bristol, Family Law, 2008) and R Schuz, 'The Impact of the United Nations Convention on the Rights of the Child on Decision-Making under the Hague Convention on the Civil Aspects of International Child Abduction' (2009 Windsor Conference) (n 47). See also Arrêté fédéral portant mise en œuvre des conventions sur l'enlèvement international d'enfants et portant approbation et mise en œuvre des Conventions de La Haye sur la protection des enfants et des adultes du 21 décembre 2007, Feuille Fédérale No 1 (2008) 33–40 RS 211.222.32 www.admin.ch/ch/f/ff/2008/33.pdf [Swiss legislation] Art 9.

[49] 2006 Responses (n 9) 107–26.

[50] Of the 1643 abducted children whose age was known, only 184 were 12 or older (11 per cent). (4 of these children were 16 and therefore the Convention should not have applied (Art 4)) 2003 Study (n 26) 27.

[51] In England the Court of Appeal held that not hearing a seven-year-old was a fundamental defect, *Re F (A Child)* [2007] EWCA 393. An Austrian court refused to recognise an order from Belgium where a five-year-old had not been heard (n 72). In Ireland it has been stated that 'anyone who has had contact with normal six year olds know that they are capable of forming their own views about many matters of direct relevance to them in their ordinary everyday life' *M. N.* [2009] (n 47) [30].

are so young as to make the process impracticable are now routinely seen by welfare officers'.[52]

The provision in the Brussels II *bis* Regulation essentially stems from the growing recognition that children as individuals have independent rights and interests which may be distinct from those of their parents and which require to be protected. Indeed, where the rights and interests of a child and his parents do not coincide the European Court of Human Rights has held that 'the child's rights must be the paramount consideration. If any balancing of interest is necessary, the interest of the child must prevail'.[53] Parents are no longer assumed necessarily to portray the interests and wishes of their children and as a result it is increasingly accepted that children should be granted the opportunity to express their own views in the interests of justice and due process.[54] However, in the Convention context questions remain. The Convention has long been criticised on the basis of a perception that the interests of the individual child are subjected to the broader interests of children as a group.[55] Similarly, application of the view that generally children should be given the opportunity to express their views in matters concerning them should not be to the detriment of the individual child caught up in the trauma of abduction within the legal peculiarities of the Convention.[56]

The fact remains that a Convention case is not a hearing on the merits, which raises three issues of concern. Firstly, the views of the child must be weighed against the underlying assumption that the child's best interests require his return. As such the child's views are 'in most cases ineffective to influence the eventual outcome'.[57] Operating a presumption that a child's views should be heard in the context of a presumption that he should nevertheless be returned, must raise a note of caution as to whether hearing the child is in his interests.[58] By analogy with the comparison between English and German cases in the early part of this decade, hearing children more frequently may not affect outcome and therefore a certain degree of caution should be exercised in hearing children whose objections may be given little weight in the light of the Convention policy of return.

[52] A Hutchinson, 'Developments in Hague Child Abduction Cases: The English Experience' (2009) *International Family Law* 186 [Hutchinson 2009].

[53] See, inter alia, *Yousef v The Netherlands* [2003] ECtHR no 33711/96. For discussion see M Potter, 'The Voice of the Child: Children's rights in Family Proceedings' (2008) *International Family Law* 140 [Potter 2008].

[54] M Weiner, 'Intolerable Situations and Counsel for Children: Following Switzerland's Example in Hague Abduction Cases' (2008) 58 *American University Law Review* 335 [Weiner 2008]; Schuz 2008 (n 37).

[55] M Freeman, 'In the Best Interests of Internationally Abducted Children? Plural, Singular, Neither' (2002) *International Family Law* 77 [Freeman 2002]. See also discussion at ch 4, II.D.

[56] 'Addressing children's rights in this individualised form, without considering the purposes of the return remedy, meant that the practicalities and the effect upon children who have been abducted have not been adequately addressed', R Lamont, 'The EU: Protecting Children's Rights in Child Abduction' (2008) *International Family Law* 110, 111.

[57] ibid 112.

[58] 'Given the summary nature of such proceedings, in which there is a presumption of return save in exceptional circumstances, beyond establishing perhaps wholesale opposition of the child, what is the purpose of hearing a child?' N Lowe, 'The Current Experiences and Difficulties of Applying Brussels II Revised' (2007) *International Family Law* 182 [Lowe 2007] 196.

Secondly, and conversely, even if following *Re D* English 'courts may in future feel somewhat less constrained in "child's objection" cases',[59] the result could be that more children are placed in the position of effective decision-maker on the basis of merely a summary hearing. In reality, by objecting to return the child is often effectively being asked to make a statement as to with which parent he wishes to reside. In usual welfare-based proceedings, children would be shielded from making such decisions. Upholding the child's objection to returning to the other State can have huge implications for the ongoing relationship between the child and the left-behind parent, who is then left to secure contact through expensive and often protracted cross-border litigation.

Thirdly, while in welfare-based proceedings children's views can assist the decision-maker and it is felt that children benefit from participating in the process,[60] in Convention cases views are only relevant if they constitute an objection to return. Where a child's views in fact coincide with the policy of return but, for example there is clear consent or acquiescence on the part of the left-behind parent, it is unlikely that the child's views would override the parents' intentions.[61] Indeed, there is some unease about hearing a child 'when the only issue at stake in the case is one of law'.[62] If views are raised which require to be ignored this can be damaging to the child. Evidence suggests that children feel let down if their views are sought but accorded little or no weight.[63] While taking account of a child's views does not mean following those views, where a child's cogent objections, or even his desire to return, are not determinative the reasons must be articulated in the judgment and to the child.[64] It is 'of importance . . . to explain to a child of appropriate age and understanding why the court is constrained to make an order for return which not infrequently causes considerable distress'.[65]

While the foregoing urges a degree of caution, it is nevertheless the position that currently children are likely to be heard routinely in Convention cases, at

[59] Potter 2008 (n 53).

[60] For discussion see N Lowe and M Murch, 'Children's Participation in the Family Justice System: Translating Principles into Practice' in J Dewar & S Parker (eds), *Family Law: Processes, Practices and Pressures* (Oxford, Hart Publishing, 2003) 9; L Elrod, 'Client-Directed Lawyers for Children: It is the "Right" Thing to Do' (2007) 27 *Pace Law Review* 869; B Rešetar and R Emery, 'Children's Rights in European Legal Proceedings: Why Are Family Practices So Different From Legal Theories?' (2008) 46 *Family Court Review* 65; M Henaghan, 'What Does a Child's Right to Be Heard in Legal Proceedings Really Mean? ABA Custody Standards Do Not Go Far Enough' [2008/2009] 42 *Family Law Quarterly* 117.

[61] At the European Judicial Network Meeting in June 2008 'the Commission agreed that it was sensible to argue that it was unnecessary to hear the child where the issue at stake was pre-abduction adult consent or post-abduction acquiescence, but added the Convention was unclear'; cited in N Lowe, 'A review of the Application of Article 11 of the Revised Brussels II Regulation' (2009) *International Family Law* 27 [Lowe 2009].

[62] M Thorpe, 'Francophone-Anglophone Judicial Conference' (2007) *International Family Law* 110 citing the resolutions of the 2007 Francophone-Anglophone Judicial Conference.

[63] An abducted child has stated that the 'major stress' was not moving country, but that the 'real problem' was the 'way decisions are made'. 'He did not think that children were taken seriously or that their views carried much weight'. M Freeman, 'International Child Abduction: the Effects' (reunite, 2006) 61. See also Daly 2009 (n 47).

[64] Daly 2009 (n 47).

[65] Potter 2008 (n 53).

least in European States. The focus of discussion therefore has to some degree shifted away from whether a child should be heard in a Convention case[66] and towards 'how this should be done',[67] with emphasis on who should hear the child and whether the child should be afforded separate representation. It is thus important to assess the implications for Convention mediation of the movement towards hearing children more frequently in Convention court hearings.

IV. The Voice of the Child in Convention Mediation

Current practice in Convention mediation has favoured the child-focused rather than the child-inclusive model and children are rarely heard.[68] Even in Germany, which has a strong tradition of hearing very young children in Convention court proceedings, 'children are only very rarely involved in mediations in Hague Convention proceedings'.[69] However, the involvement of children in Convention mediation is being advocated,[70] and the development of child-inclusive domestic mediation and the change in practice in Convention court proceedings are bound to have an influence.

Indeed, as Convention mediation is here viewed as one aspect of the broader procedure for handling a Convention application, it may be necessary, at least in intra-European Union cases, to ensure that children are given the opportunity to be heard. Convention mediation as defined and described in this book should be perceived as part of the 'proceedings' which, at least in the context of the Brussels II *bis* Regulation, requires that the age-appropriate and mature child is given opportunity to express his views. Additionally, a court asked to grant a consent order in the terms of an agreement reached in mediation may only be able to do so if the child was given an opportunity to be heard.[71] Alternatively it may be important to ensure that the child had the opportunity to be heard so as not to prejudice recognition and enforcement of the order in another State.[72] In this regard both the 1996 Hague Convention and the Brussels II *bis* Regulation allow a State to refuse to recognise an order if it was given, except in case of urgency,

[66] For discussion of the position in England and Wales following *Re D* [2006] (n 43) see Baroness Hale of Richmond, 'The Voice of the Child' (2007) *International Family Law* 171; Freeman & Hutchinson 2007 (n 30); M Freeman and A Hutchinson, 'Abduction and the Voice of the Child: *Re M* and After' (2008) *International Family Law* 163; H Setright, E Devereux, and A Hutchinson, 'Discretion, Settlement and Child's Objections: *Re M (Abduction)*' (2008) *Family Law* 230; McEleavy 2008 (n 30); Hutchinson 2009 (n 52); Lowe 2009 (n 61).

[67] *Re D* [2006] (n 43) 59.

[68] Questionnaire Responses (ch 1, n 24) BAFM; Judge Carl; Judge Olland.

[69] ibid, Judge Carl.

[70] ibid.

[71] ibid, Austrian Central Authority.

[72] In *Eugenie* (2006) the Austrian court refused to recognise and enforce a Belgian decision because the views of a five-year-old had not been sought, Lowe 2007 (n 58) n 29.

without the child having been given an opportunity to be heard.[73] However, under the 1996 Hague Convention, a State can only refuse recognition on the basis that the child was not heard 'in the context of a judicial or administrative proceeding',[74] which may exclude mediated agreements which are simply confirmed by a court. Indeed according to the Explanatory Report 'it was pointed out, with good reason, that it is not always in the interests of the child to have to give an opinion, in particular if the two parents are in agreement on the measure to be taken'.[75]

While one of the fundamental facets and benefits of mediation is that it minimises the interference of the State and promotes party autonomy, the reality in Convention mediation is that the authorities of the State are to an extent already engaged as a result of the application having been made. As such, while in domestic family mediation there may be justification for not hearing the child and instead assisting the parents to maintain their parental decision-making roles, in the Convention context it seems sensible that a decision on whether or not the child should be heard is not left to the parents but is rather viewed in the light of the Convention application. Indeed, where an invitation to hear the child is given to the parents, experience has shown that 'few parents make use of this offer.'[76] Additionally, it should be remembered that where mediation enables parents to resolve the dispute there will be no subsequent intervention at which the child's voice would be heard and therefore providing such an opportunity in the context of the Convention proceedings is even more important.

Consequently, it is suggested that a decision as to whether a child should be heard should be taken in the context of the Convention procedure, rather than as a specific element of the mediation or court processes. Viewing the voice of the child in this way reflects the fact that whether the parents opt to mediate or litigate, they do so in the shadow of the Convention application. Additionally, this means that the decision is taken at the outset of the proceedings, in line with English jurisprudence that 'European cases require the court to address at the outset whether and how the child is to be given the opportunity of being heard'.[77] A subsequent decision of the Court of Appeal held that whether and how the court will hear the child should be considered at its first directions hearing.[78]

Assessing at the outset of the proceedings whether a child should be heard will manifest itself in different ways in different States. Where there is a preliminary ruling prior to mediation or litigation, as in England and Wales, the court can decide at this juncture whether the child should be heard. Where the Central

[73] Convention on Jurisdiction, Applicable Law, Recognition, Enforcement and Co-operation in respect of Parental Responsibility and Measures for the Protection of Children (adopted 19 October 1996, entered into force 1 January 2002) 35 ILM 1391 [1996 Hague Convention] Art 23(2)(b); Brussels II *bis* Regulation (n 42) Art 23(b).

[74] Art 23(2)(b).

[75] P Lagarde, 'Explanatory Report' in *Actes et documents de la dix-huitième session, Tome II, Protection des enfants* (The Hague, Hague Conference, 1996) 514 [Lagarde Report] [585].

[76] Questionnaire Responses (ch 1, n 24) BAFM.

[77] *Re D* [2006] (n 43) 61.

[78] *Re F (Abduction: Child's Wishes)* [2007] EWCA 468 [2].

Authority can pass the case directly to mediation, as in Switzerland, that authority or the mediators at an initial intake session can make a decision on whether the child should be heard.[79] Where the court hears the case prior to mediation, such as might occur in Germany, the court as the first intervener can decide whether the child should be heard. The different procedures in different States mean that it is impossible to suggest one model for hearing children. Indeed both the United Nations Convention[80] and the Brussels II *bis* Regulation[81] leave the manner in which a child should be heard to national law. However, notwithstanding that the methodology will differ from State to State, it is proposed that three principles are needed to facilitate hearing the child.

Firstly, appropriate mechanisms for hearing children need to be established. A result of the Brussels II *bis* Regulation and the jurisprudence flowing from it is that European Union States which have traditionally not heard children routinely in Convention proceedings must establish procedures to meet the increased workload. Viewing the voice of the child in the context of the Convention application regardless of whether the parents opt to mediate or litigate will allow expertise to develop, speed up the process and ensure that all children receive the same standard of service. Additionally, as the purpose of hearing a child in domestic welfare-based proceedings or family mediation differs from in Convention proceedings, establishing mechanisms specifically for Convention applications allows the voice of the child to be heard within the appropriate context. For example, the child can be informed of the particular nature of Convention proceedings and consulted primarily on the basis of whether he objects to return, or whether his views establish any other exceptions to return. Procedural questions of costs, avoidance of delay and methods of hearing a child all need to be considered and it is suggested that further study also needs to be undertaken on whether children should be separately represented in Convention proceedings.[82]

[79] Swiss legislation (n 48) Arts 3 and 4.

[80] Art 12(2).

[81] Recital 19.

[82] Separate representation of the child is now mandatory in Switzerland, Swiss legislation (n 48) Art 9(3). In South Africa all children have a constitutional right to representation at the State's expense, South African Constitution 1996 § 28(1)(h), 2006 Responses (n 9) 121. For discussion see P von Dadelszen, 'Legal Representation of the Child in International Child Abduction Cases' (2009) *International Family Law* 152; Weiner 2008 (n 54); P von Dadelszen, 'The Lawyer for the Child in New Zealand' (2007) *International Family Law* 129; P Boshier, 'Care and Protection of Children: New Zealand and Australian Experience of Cross-Border Co-operation' (4th World Congress on Family Law and Children's Rights, Cape Town, South Africa, March 2005) [Boshier 2005]; W Keough, 'The Separate Representation of Children in Australian Family Law: Effective Practice or Mere Rhetoric?' (2002) 19 *Canadian Journal of Family Law* 371. For a contrary English view see *Re H (Abduction)* [2006] EWCA 1247, discussed in McEleavy 2008 (n 30). A concern regarding separate representation is the costs involved and the potential for delay, see P Beaumont and P McEleavy, *The Hague Convention on International Child Abduction* (Oxford, Oxford University Press, 1999) [Beaumont & McEleavy] 187; *Re C (Abduction: Separate Representation of Children)* [2008] EWHC 517; and McGuinness 2009 (n 47) 18. It is also suggested in the *General Principles and Guide to Good Practice on Transfrontier Contact Concerning Children* (Bristol, Family Law, 2008) 36 that children should be represented in mediation where the issue is contact rather than return.

Secondly, a report should be prepared on the child's views, which is accessible to all appropriate professionals. Thus if mediation is attempted but fails to lead to agreement, the judge has access to the child's views without the need to hear the child again. Alternatively if the judge is asked to formalise an agreement he can be aware of the child's views prior to granting a court order in the terms of the agreement. The existence of a report prepared at the outset means that the child does not need to be heard multiple times by multiple professionals. There may be occasions, however, where a judge or mediator wishes to hear the child directly notwithstanding the existence of the report. For example a judge may hear a child if there is doubt as to the child's maturity, or simply because judicial hearing of children is entrenched in the particular legal system.[83] A mediator may hear a child where the parents have reached agreement on additional substantive issues and therefore no further intervention is envisaged, and the child has not been consulted on these issues. It is suggested that these cases where the child is heard a second time in addition to the report should remain unusual. However, the advantage of a report is that it does not preclude the judge or mediator from requesting to see the child directly in the appropriate case.

The report should be available to relevant Convention professionals but not directly to the parents. Following practice in usual domestic mediation the mediator should feed-back to the parents. This is important to protect the confidentiality of a child's views and to protect the child in the light of the familial nature of the dispute. Children should retain the right to state which if any of their views they wish their parents to hear. A child must be allowed to express views that he would like a judge to be aware of if decision-making responsibility falls to the judge, but would not like his parents to know. The professional charged with hearing the child should make this distinction clear to the child.

Thirdly, the outcome of the proceedings should be explained to the child who has participated, particularly where the outcome is not in line with his expressed views.[84]

In the reunite scheme a hybrid approach similar to what is advocated here was adopted. This project took place prior to *Re D* at a stage when children were still rarely heard in Convention proceedings in England. In appropriate cases the court, which was seized having given a preliminary ruling, was asked to 'direct that the child be interviewed'.[85] Thus the mediators were the ones who referred

[83] The issue of whether a judge must directly hear a child in Convention proceedings arose before the European Court of Human Rights in *Maumousseau and Washington v France* [2007] ECtHR no 39388/05. The Court held that it was not its role to review the interpretation and application of the provisions of international conventions other than in cases of an 'arbitrary' decision, recognising that States enjoy a 'margin of appreciation' and avoiding stating that the judge must hear the child. In making this decision the Court at 77–80 referred to its previous decision in *Eskinazi and Chellouche v Turkey* [2005] ECtHR no 14600/05. For discussion see P Beaumont, 'The Jurisprudence of the European Court of Human Rights and the European Court of Justice on the Hague Convention on International Child Abduction' in *Recueil des cours: volume 335 (2008)* (Leiden, Martinus Nijhoff Publishers, 2009) [Beaumont 2009] 64–5.

[84] See Parkinson 2006 (n 2) 483; Daly 2009 (n 47).

[85] reunite, 'Mediation in International Parental Child Abduction: The reunite Mediation Pilot Scheme' (October 2006) www.reunite.org/edit/files/Mediation%20Report.pdf [reunite Report] 10.

the child to be heard but the means by which the child was actually heard reflected court practice. The court was asked to direct an interview of the child in the same way, and using the same professionals, as in a Convention court hearing. A report was then filed with the court and provided to the mediator, although unlike what is suggested here it was also available to the parents.

The foregoing demonstrates that viewing mediation as part of the broader Convention application ensures that mechanisms can be established to hear the child's views notwithstanding that in domestic family mediation this remains unusual practice. It is also suggested that a particular advantage of mediation over court proceedings in the Convention context is that concerns regarding the voice of the child are diminished and the positive effects of hearing the child increase.

Concerns are diminished because parents in mediation are not constrained by the return mechanism and thus the views of the child do not need to be weighed against the presumption of return. Equally, the views of the child can be taken into account even if they do not constitute an objection to return. There are additional positive effects to hearing a child whose parents mediate as the child's views, although sought in the context of the Convention application, are not restricted to merely the issue of return but can influence the exercise of future contact between a child and his non-resident parent. In this way the views of the child have greater potential to influence decision-making and the child's participation is thus more meaningful, which is surely in the interests of children. The option to mediate thus also offers a response to the concern that the rights and interests of the individual child are not sufficiently addressed in application of the Convention.[86]

V. Conclusion

As a result of the Brussels II *bis* Regulation children are being heard more often in Convention proceedings than has traditionally been the case and this trend is likely to continue. Indeed almost all children are now routinely heard in some States, even though the provision in the Regulation imports an age and maturity gateway. It is suggested that careful consideration is given to the threshold for age and maturity. It would seem logical to apply the same test to both the Brussels II bis Regulation and the Convention so that children who are considered too young or immature to have their views taken into account for the purposes of Article 13(2) of the Convention should not be heard. In this regard it should be remembered that most abducted children are very young.[87]

The current practice in some States of routinely hearing very young children, notwithstanding that their views in many cases will carry little or no weight is

[86] ch 4, II.D.

[87] 2003 Study (n 26) 27–8.

unsatisfactory. It is suggested that empirical research be undertaken on the effects on children of the Regulation provision, and the weight that courts are actually attaching to children's views. Following such research the practice of routinely hearing very young children in the context of a Convention application may need to be revisited.

However, where a child is of an appropriate age to be consulted mechanisms should be established to enable this decision to be made at the outset in the context of the Convention application, whether the parents opt to mediate or litigate. By making a decision at the outset and using expeditious mechanisms it can be ensured that hearing the child does not cause delay. The professional hearing the child might be a welfare officer, a mediator or a judge depending on the process in the particular State and it should be ensured that this professional is adequately trained and seeks the child's views in the context of the Convention application. It is also necessary that a report is prepared to ensure that other professionals have access to the views of the child. Finally, mechanisms should be established to ensure that once the proceedings are over the child is made aware of the decision and how the decision-makers took account of his views.

While these procedures apply whether the parents mediate or litigate, an important advantage of Convention mediation over the alternative court process is that the voice of the child can have a greater impact. The parents are not constrained by the return mechanism and thus the child's expressed views are able to have a greater influence on decision-making. This ensures that the child's participation in the process is more meaningful, and he is protected from the burden of inappropriate responsibility, as only those views which he wishes his parents to know will be shared with them. Overall, the potential negative effects of hearing the child in the context of the Convention are minimised and the potential positive effects of including the child in the process are enhanced. Thus Convention mediation can offer great value to the current regime in the context of the growing understanding of the importance of the voice of the child.

6

Conclusions

I. From Enthusiasm . . .

Enthusiasm surrounding the use of mediation as a means to handle Convention applications is well-founded given the potential advantages as outlined above. Principally, mediation offers parents an alternative to the court process which can be more adaptable to their particular needs and circumstances and can thus better take account of the individual interests of their child. Specifically, parents can take a broader look at the situation and seek to resolve the question of the child's future place of residence by discussing the broader issues which impact upon that decision, but which would fall outside the scope of the Convention court hearing. As a result mediation offers a response to certain concerns regarding the application of the Convention in the present day and thereby provides a means through which Contracting States can improve their implementation and operation of the Convention in the interests of families.

In the now typical case where the left-behind father either does not want, or is unlikely to be granted, the primary care of the child, mediation offers parents the opportunity to negotiate ongoing contact arrangements. These arrangements can then be drawn up as an enforceable court order providing legal certainty for all parties. Where parents can reach agreement on the child's future place of residence and ongoing contact arrangements they can resolve the dispute in one step rather than the two steps envisaged by the Convention. The potential saving of time and costs and, more importantly, the prevention of further disruption to the child poses a major advantage to the current regime. Alternatively where parties cannot agree on a permanent place of residence or recognise that the child should return, the mediation process allows them to negotiate welfare issues which may otherwise form a barrier to return. Furthermore, as such an agreement can be turned into an enforceable order the returning parent can rely upon it. This creates greater protection than is currently available through the attachment of unenforceable undertakings or conditions.

In addition to the advantages as to outcome, there are various benefits inherent in the mediation process itself. Firstly, the mediation process can offer a more child-friendly approach. Through mediation parents maintain autonomy to craft solutions in the interests of their particular child. This responds to the concern that the Convention does not pay sufficient regard to the rights and interests of the individual child in the individual case. As parents are not constrained to apply the return mechanism in the absence of a viable exception, the views of the age-appropriate child can also be fully considered, and in appropriate cases may have greater influence than would be possible in the alternative court hearing. This ensures the child's participation is more satisfactory, which responds to concerns regarding hearing a child against the backdrop of the presumption of return. It also ensures the child's participation is more meaningful and is not merely paying lip-service to the child's right to be heard. Secondly, there are benefits inherent in the process which have value beyond the resolution of the abduction. The mediation process can improve communication and reduce conflict, and ensures parents maintain responsibility for decision-making. These benefits have longer-term value potentially impacting how the parents resolve future disputes, which is particularly important in the Convention context where abducted children tend to be very young.[1]

In the light of the foregoing it is not surprising that Convention mediation is enthusiastically endorsed by certain legislatures, judges and experts in the field.

II. . . . To Action

Despite the advantages outlined above and discussed in detail throughout this book, and notwithstanding the impressive and successful initiatives undertaken by some States, authorities and organisations, the majority of Convention applications currently fall outside a mediatory regime. Enthusiasm and increased discussion about the use of mediation has not led to much action in the field. In the broader cross-border context, it has been stated that: '[m]ediation is still a bit like climate change: Everybody talks about it, but nobody seems willing to do something about it'.[2] However, research conducted by this author highlighted that in fact what is lacking is not necessarily a willingness to move forward, but rather a clear understanding of how this might be done.

This book has therefore primarily sought to provide an overview of what mediation is and how it can fit within the constraints of the Convention, with a view to moving from enthusiasm to action. At this early stage of the development of the discipline it has been necessary to offer a broad overview rather than focusing on specific aspects in more depth. Particularly this book has provided a working description of mediation, which offers clarity and thereby seeks to prevent further discussion proceeding at cross-purposes. Additionally, it has outlined how the

[1] N Lowe, 'A Statistical Analysis of Applications made in 2003 under the Hague Convention of 25 October 1980 on the Civil Aspects of International Child Abduction: Part I: Overall Report' Prel. Doc. No 3/2006 (2007 update) http://hcch.e-vision.nl/upload/wop/abd_pd03e1_2007.pdf 2008, 27-8.

[2] Y Heijmans and E Plasschaert, 'Effective Cross-border Mediation in Europe' (2006) *European Briefings*.

mediation process can operate as a means of applying the Convention. Viewing mediation in this way, as one aspect of the broader procedure, means that it is supported by adequate legal structures which provide appropriate safeguards. Moreover, situating the mediation process within this general procedure ensures that where mediation is not appropriate in the specific circumstances, or fails to lead to agreement on the child's place of residence, the application can pass expeditiously into the court system to be resolved on the basis of the Convention without 'undue delay'. As a technique for applying the Convention the mediation process can also benefit from any advantageous regime operating in the context of the Convention, as well as the already considerable co-operative structures existing between networks of Central Authorities and judges. Additionally, by developing a mediation process within the procedure for handling applications, mediation offers advantages to parents whilst still respecting and indeed supporting the operation of the Convention.

This book has also outlined some of the legal, procedural and practical questions which had previously not been discussed in any detail. Particular emphasis has been placed on those areas which would benefit from agreement at the international level so that mediation can develop harmoniously. It is recognised that if States are to embrace the use of mediation they need to be involved in the process of development and therefore key issues have been highlighted and solutions suggested as a basis for further discussion. Notably, it is suggested that Convention mediation should be developed as a distinct discipline given that the context requires it to operate in a significantly different way to more general family mediation. A specialist system can take account of, inter alia, the need for expeditious action; the particular relationship between the mediation process and the court process in the Convention context; and confidentiality requirements. Additionally, structures can be established for hearing the age-appropriate child; ensuring his views are made available to all necessary professionals; and providing feedback to the child once an outcome is reached. Additionally, mediators can be required to undertake additional training in order to be entered on a register of Convention mediators. Thus States can be confident in the quality of mediators and expertise can develop.

Whilst it is the intention to promote international acceptance of the use of Convention mediation and encourage harmonious development by providing a basis for further discussion, an additional advantage of mediation is that in practical terms it can continue to develop on a State-by-State basis. Its development requires no legislative amendments, at least at the international level, and while certain elements of the mediation process may benefit from being enshrined in any future Protocol to the Convention, and a Good Practice Guide will be beneficial, States can proceed to introduce a mediation scheme as soon as they have a viable system and adequately trained mediators. Certainly some States with more experience in mediation may be able to introduce Convention mediation with relative ease and speed notwithstanding that certain other States may not yet be in a position to do so.

The Convention has always provided inspiration for the development of novel mechanisms and structures to support its operation and enhance cross-border co-operation, from the establishment of the network of Central Authorities in the instrument itself to the many 'post-Convention services' which have evolved in the years since its entry into force. Against this pioneering background it should not be surprising that the use of mediation to facilitate the resolution of cross-border disputes concerning children is primarily being discussed in the context of this Convention. Significantly, many of these mechanisms and structures have subsequently been utilised in the context of other Hague Conventions and it should be expected that the development of Convention mediation will similarly act as a catalyst for its broader use. Consequently, the issues addressed in this book have importance initially in the immediate context, but additionally as a starting point for future broader endeavours.

The Convention is a successful instrument. It has been in force for more than a quarter of a century, attracted over 80 Contracting States, and has offered a solution to thousands of families caught up in the trauma of abduction. The challenge for Contracting States in the light of social and demographic changes is to continue to implement and apply the Convention in a way that best meets the needs of those it is designed to protect. It has been demonstrated in this book that in appropriate cases mediation can provide a means through which the needs of families are better met and therefore the willingness to move forward with the development of the discipline is justified. This book has sought to turn goodwill into good practice by defining mediation and outlining how it can fit within the constraints of the Convention, as well as highlighting the added value that mediation offers. It is submitted that the time is ripe to move from enthusiasm about the use of Convention mediation and towards greater actual practice in the interests of better supporting families.

Appendix

Questionnaire on Mediation in the Context of the Hague Convention on International Child Abduction

Hague Convention Procedure

1. Is mediation offered in all cases and if not what criteria are used to establish which cases are considered suitable for mediation?
2. How and by whom are parties referred to mediation?
3. At what stage in the proceedings is mediation offered? Specifically, is there an initial hearing in court before mediation can commence?
4. Does mediation take place with both parties in the requested State or can mediation proceed with parties and mediators working in different States?
5. How can mediation fit within the time frame of a Hague Convention application? Are there specific procedures to allow for expedition? Has this been effective?
6. How is it ensured that a decision to mediate is not construed as acquiescence under the Convention?
7. If an agreement is not reached are the parties able to institute court proceedings expeditiously and what is the procedure for this?

Content of Mediation

8. Are parties informed of the likely outcome of their Convention application if they were to proceed through the courts, and is this the background against which mediation takes place?
9. Does mediation focus purely on whether or not the child should be returned or are parties able to discuss other broader issues relating to, inter alia, custody and contact?
10. Do you have experience of mediating the conditions for return so that the abducting parent feels comfortable to return to the State of habitual residence? Please describe how effective you think this was?

11. Do parties have the opportunity to discuss any agreements with their legal representatives before committing to them?
12. Are mediation sessions confidential and do you have any comments on the issue of confidentiality?

The Child

13. How, if at all, is the child involved in the mediation process? How, if at all, are the views of the child ascertained?
14. What if any arrangements are made for contact between the child and the left behind parent during the mediation process?

Recognition and Enforcement of Mediated Agreements

15. If an agreement is reached, what is the process for making this agreement enforceable?
16. Do you have any information on whether or not mediated agreements have been recognised or if necessary enforced in a foreign State?
17. Do you have experience of mediated agreements emanating from other States which have been registered or, if necessary, enforced in your State? What was the procedure for this?

The Mediators

18. Who undertakes the mediation, and what training and qualifications have the mediator(s) received?
19. How many mediators are involved in a case? Is it considered necessary to have a mediator from each State?

General Comments

20. Do you have any other comments on the use of mediation in the context of the Child Abduction Convention?

BIBLIOGRAPHY

Books

Bainham, A (ed), *The International Survey of Family Law* 2005 edn (Bristol, Family Law, 2005).

Beaumont, P and McEleavy, P, *The Hague Convention on International Child Abduction* (Oxford, Oxford University Press, 1999).

Fisher, R, Ury, W and Patton, B, *Getting to Yes – Negotiating an agreement without giving in*, 2nd edn (London, Random House, 1991).

Freeman, M (ed), *Children's Rights: A Comparative Perspective* (Aldershot, Dartmouth Publishing, 1996).

Fulchiron, H (ed), *Les enlèvements d'enfants à travers les frontières* (Brussels, Bruylant, 2004).

Fulchiron, H and Nourissat, C (eds), *Le nouveau droit communautaire du divorce et de la responsabilité parentale* (Paris, Dalloz, 2005).

Greif, G and Hegar, R, *When Parents Kidnap: The families behind the headlines* (New York, The Free Press, 1993).

Hall Dick, A and Ballantine, T, *The Art of Family Law: Skills for Successful Practice* (Edinburgh, Sweet & Maxwell, 2001).

Hodson, D, *A Practical Guide to International Family Law* (Wiltshire, Family Law, 2008).

Lowe, L, Everall, M and Nicholls, M, *International Movement of Children: Law, Practice and Procedure* (Bristol, Family Law, 2003).

Parkinson, L, *Family Mediation* (London, Sweet & Maxwell, 1997).

Westcott, J (ed), *Family Mediation – Past, Present and Future* (Bristol, Family Law, 2004).

Chapters in Books

Bainham, A, 'Contact as a Right and Obligation' in A Bainham et al (eds), *Children and Their Families: Contact Rights and Welfare* (Oxford, Hart Publishing, 2003).

Beaumont, P, 'European Court of Human Rights Cases Concerning The Hague Convention on International Child Abduction' in *The Jurisprudence of the European Court of Human Rights and the European Court of Justice on the Hague Convention on International Child Abduction* (Leiden, Martinus Nijhoff Publishers, 2009).

Bucher, A, 'l'intérêt de l'enfant pénètre la convention sur l'enlèvement' in *Vers de nouveaux équilibres entre ordres juridiques, Liber amicorum Hélène Gaudemet-Tallon*, (Paris, Dalloz, 2008).

Demars, S, 'L'enlèvement parental international' in J Renchon (ed), *L'enfant et les relations familiales internationales* (Brussels, Bruylant, 2003).

Duncan, W, 'Cross-frontier Contact between Children and their Parents: Identifying the Problems' in G Miller (ed), *Frontiers of Family Law* (Aldershot, Ashgate Publishing, 2003).

Hunt, J, 'Intervening in Litigated Contact: Ideas from Other Jurisdictions' in M Maclean (ed), *Parenting after Partnering: Containing Conflict After Separation* (Oxford, Hart Publishing, 2007).

Kelly, J, 'Legal and Educational Interventions for Families in Residence and Contact Disputes' in J Dewar and S Parker (eds), *Family Law: Processes, Practices and Pressures* (Oxford, Hart Publishing, 2003).

Lowe, N and Murch, M, 'Children's Participation in the Family Justice System: Translating Principles into Practice' in J Dewar and S Parker (eds), *Family Law: Processes, Practices and Pressures* (Oxford, Hart Publishing, 2003).

Murch, M, 'The Cross-disciplinary Approach to Family Law – Trying to Mix Oil with Water?' in A Bainham, D Pearl and R Pickford (eds), *Frontiers of Family Law*, 2nd edn (United Kingdom, John Wiley and Sons, 1995).

Ngabonziza, D, 'La médiation dans les disputes familiales internationals – Le rôle futur des Conventions de la Haye' in S Detrick and P Vlaardingerbroek (eds), *Globalization of Child Law – The Role of the Hague Conventions* (The Hague, Martinus Nijhoff Publishers, 1999).

Schuz, R, 'The Hague Child Abduction Convention and the United Nations Convention on the Rights of the Child' in P Lødrup and E Modvar (eds), *Family Life and Human Rights* (Oslo, Gyldendal, 2004).

—— 'The Voice of the Child in the Israeli Family Court' in B Atkin and F Banda, *The International Survey of Family Law* (Bristol, Family Law, 2008).

—— 'Protection Versus Autonomy: The Child Abduction Experience' in Y Ronen and C Greenbaum (eds), *The Case for the Child: Towards a New Agenda* (Antwerp, Intersentia, 2008).

Shone, M, 'Law, Relational Ethics and the Resolution of Custody and Access Disputes' in P Lødrup and E Modvar (eds), *Family Life and Human Rights* (Oslo, Gyldendal, 2004).

Smart, C, 'Children and the Transformation of Family Law' in J Dewar and S Parker (eds), *Family Law: Processes, Practices and Pressures* (Oxford, Hart Publishing, 2003).

Smith, D, 'Making Contact Work in International Cases: Promoting Contact Whilst Preventing International Parental Abduction' in A Bainham et al (eds), *Children and Their Families: Contact Rights and Welfare* (Oxford, Hart Publishing, 2003).

Wilkins, R, 'International Law, Social Change and the Family' in P Lødrup and E Modvar (eds), *Family Life and Human Rights* (Oslo, Gyldendal, 2004).

Articles

Abramson, H, 'Selecting Mediators and Representing Clients in Cross-Cultural Disputes' (2006) 7.2 *Cardozo Journal of Conflict Resolution* 253.

Achim, J, Cyr, F and Filion, L, 'L'implication de l'enfant en médiation familiale: de la théorie à la pratique' (1997) 18:1 *Revue québécoise de psychologie* 41.

Alanen, J, 'When Human Rights Conflict: Mediating International Parental Kidnapping Disputes Involving the Domestic Violence Defense' (2008) 40 *University of Miami Inter-American Law Review* 49.

Anton, A, 'The Hague Convention on International Child Abduction' (1981) 30 *ICLQ* 537.

Arcaro, T, 'Creating a Legal Society in the Western Hemisphere to Support the Hague Convention on the Civil Aspects of International Child Abduction' (2008) 40 *University of Miami Inter-American Law Review* 109.

Armstrong, S, 'Is the Jurisdiction of England and Wales Correctly Applying the 1980 Hague Convention on the Civil Aspects of International Child Abduction?' (2002) 51 *ICLQ* 427.

Baker, H, 'The International Family Justice Judicial Conference for Common Law and Commonwealth Jurisdictions' (2009) *International Family Law* 250.

Barton, C, 'ADR Professional: Becoming a Family Mediator: Out in the Real World' (2007) *Family Law* 942.

Bateman, J, 'Brussels Bulletin: a New European Framework' (2008) *International Family Law* 49.

Bentch, S, 'Court-Sponsored Custody Mediation to Prevent Parental Kidnapping: A Disarmament Proposal' [1986-87] 18 *St Mary's Law Journal* 361.

Bercovitch, J, 'Mediation Success or Failure: A Search for the Elusive Criteria' (2006) 7.2 *Cardozo Journal of Conflict Resolution* 289.

Bondesen, E, 'Cross-Cultural Mediation – A Challenge'.

Boshier, P, 'Contact and Relocation: Some Reflections on a Changing World' (2007) 12 *Judges' Newsletter* 41.

—— 'International Family Justice from a New Zealand Perspective' (2008) *International Family Law* 149.

Bradley, C, 'European Harmonisation and the EU Constitution' (2005) *Family Law* 645.

Bramwell, L, 'ADR Professional: The UK College of Family Mediators' (2008) *Family Law* 172.

Bruch, C, 'And How are the Children? The Effects of Ideology and Mediation on Child Custody Law and Children's Well-being in the United States' (1988) 2 *International Journal of Law and the Family* 106.

—— 'Religious Law, Secular Practice and Child's Human Rights in Child Abduction Cases under the Hague Child Abduction Convention' (2000) 33 *New York University Journal of International Law & Politics* 49.

—— 'Sound Research of Wishful Thinking in Child Custody Cases? Lessons from Relocation Law' (2006) 40 *Family Law Quarterly* 281.

Bryant, D, 'Judicial Communication' (2007) *International Family Law* 199.

Bucher, A, 'The New Swiss Federal Act on International Child Abduction' (2008) 4 *Journal of Private International Law* 139.

Carl, E and Eschweiler, P, 'Hearing of a Child – Risks and Chances' (unpublished – on file with author).

Carl, E and Wicke, C, 'Mediation Projects in Hague Cases: Developments in Germany' (2007) 12 *Judges' Newsletter* 49.

Carl, E, Copin, J and Ripke, L, 'Le projet pilote franco-allemand de médiation familiale professionnelle: Un modèle de collaboration internationale dans le cadre de conflits familiaux' (2004) *Kind-Prax Special* 25.

Chiancone, J, Girdner, L and Hoff, P, 'Issues in Resolving Cases of International Child Abduction by Parents' (December 2001) *Juvenile Justice Bulletin*.

Coester-Waltjen, D, 'The Future of the Hague Child Abduction Convention: The Rise of Domestic and International Tensions – The European Perspective' (2000) 33 *New York University Journal of International Law & Politics* 59.

Daly, A, 'Considered or Merely Heard? The Views of Young Children in Hague Convention Cases in Ireland' (2009) 1 *Irish Journal of Family Law* 16.

De Silva, S, 'The International Parental Child Abduction Service of the International Social Service Australian Branch' (2006) 11 *Judges' Newsletter* 61.

Duncan, W, 'Action in Support of the Hague Child Abduction Convention: A view from the Permanent Bureau' (2000) 33 *New York University Journal of International Law & Politics* 103.

Elrod, L, 'Client-Directed Lawyers for Children: It is the "Right" Thing to Do' (2007) 27 *Pace Law Review* 869.

Emery, R, 'Easing the Pain of Divorce for Children: Children's Voices, Causes of Conflict, and Mediation – Comments on Kelly's "Resolving Child Custody Disputes" ' (2002) 10 *Virginia Journal of Social Policy & Law* 164.

Emery, R et al, 'Child Custody Mediation and Litigation: Custody, Contact, and Coparenting 12 Years After Initial Dispute Resolution' (2001) 69 *Journal of Consulting & Clinical Psychology* 323.

Emery, R, Matthews, S and Kitzmann, K, 'Child Custody Mediation and Litigation: Parents' Satisfaction and Functioning One Year after Settlement' (1994) 62 *Journal of Consulting & Clinical Psychology* 124.

Emery, R, Sbarra, D and Grover, T, 'Divorce Mediation: Research and Reflections' (2005) 43 *Family Court Review* 22.

Fiorini, A, 'Enlèvements internationaux d'enfants – soluions internationales et responsabilités étatiques' (2006) 51 *McGill Law Journal* 279.

Freeman, M, 'Primary Carers and the Hague Child Abduction Convention' (2001) *International Family Law* 140.

—— 'In the Best Interests of Internationally Abducted Children? Plural, Singular, Neither' (2002) *International Family Law* 77.

—— 'Outcomes for Abducted Children' (2004) *International Family Law* 171.

—— 'Effects of International Child Abduction on Children' (2006) *International Family Law* 129.

—— and A Hutchinson, 'The Voice of the Child in International Child Abduction' (2007) *International Family Law* 177.

—— and A Hutchinson, 'Abduction and the Voice of the Child: *Re M* and After' (2008) *International Family Law* 163.

——, A Hutchinson and H Setright, 'Child Abduction – A Role for Mediation?' (2002) *International Family Law* 104.

—— and H Setright, 'The Hague Child Abduction Convention: Current Developments in Hague Convention Jurisprudence or "A Universal Vaccine for a Mutating Virus?" ' [2002/203] 6 *Contemporary Issues in Law* 279.

Funken, K, 'Comparative Dispute Management: Court-connected Mediation in Japan and Germany' (2002) 3 *German Law Journal.*

Garwood, F, 'Children in Conciliation: The Experience of Involving Children in Conciliation' (1990) *Family & Conciliation Courts Review* 43.

George, R, 'Practitioners' Approaches to Child Welfare after Parental Separation: an Anglo-French Comparison' (2007) *Child and Family Law Quarterly* 337.

Gold, J, 'ADR Through a Cultural Lens: How Cultural Values Shape our Disputing Processes' (2005) *Journal of Dispute Resolution* 289.

Greene, A, 'Seen and Not Heard?: Children's Objections Under the Hague Convention on International Child Abduction' (2005) 13 *University of Miami International & Comparative Law Review* 105.

Greif, G, 'Many Years after the Parental Abduction: Some Consequences of Relevance to the Court System' (1998) 36 *Family & Conciliation Courts Review* 32.

—— 'A Parental Report on the Long-Term Consequences for Children of Abduction by the Other Parent' (2000) 31(1) *Child Psychiatry & Human Development* 59.

Hale, B, 'The Voice of the Child' (2007) *International Family Law* 171.

Hayes, S, 'ADR Professional: Redefining Practice: Lessons Learned as a Researcher and Mediator' (2007) *Family Law* 844.

Heijmans, Y and Plasschaert, E, 'Effective Cross-border Mediation in Europe' (2006) *European Briefings, Association of Corporate Counsel.*

Henaghan, M, 'What Does a Child's Right to Be Heard in Legal Proceedings Really Mean? ABA Custody Standards Do Not Go Far Enough' [2008/09] 42 *Family Law Quarterly* 117.

Hodson, D, 'European Family Law – An Expanding Regime?' (2005) *International Family Law* 235.

—— 'The EU Mediation Directive: The European Encouragement to Family Law ADR' (2008) *International Family Law* 209.

Hutchinson, A, 'Developments in Hague Child Abduction Cases: The English Experience' (2009) *International Family Law* 186.

James, A, James, A and McNamee, S, 'Research: Turn Down the Volume? Not Hearing Children in Family Proceedings' (2004) *Child and Family Law Quarterly* 189.

Johnston, J et al, 'Early Identification of Risk Factors for Parental Abduction' *Juvenile Justice Bulletin* (March 2001).

Kelly, J, 'Psychological and Legal Interventions for Parents and Children in Custody and Access Disputes: Current Research and Practice' (2002) 10 *Virginia Journal of Social Policy & Law* 129.

—— 'Family Mediation Research: Is There Empirical Support for the Field?' (2004) 22 *Conflict Resolution Quarterly* 3.

Keough, W, 'The Separate Representation of Children in Australian Family Law – Effective Practice or Mere Rhetoric?' (2002) 19 *Canadian Journal of Family Law* 371.

Kilkelly, U and Lundy, L, 'Children's Rights in Action: Using the UN Convention on the Rights of the Child as an Auditing Tool' (2006) *Child and Family Law Quarterly* 331.

Koopman, E et al, 'Professional Perspectives on Court-Connected Child Custody Mediation' (1991) 29 *Family Court Review* 304.

Lamont, R, 'The EU: Protecting Children's Rights in Child Abduction' (2008) *International Family Law* 110.

Lowe, N, 'The Current Experiences and Difficulties of Applying Brussels II Revised' (2007) *International Family Law* 182.

—— 'A Review of the Application of Article 11 of the Revised Brussels II Regulation' (2009) *International Family Law* 27.

– – and Horosova, K, 'The Operation of the 1980 Hague Abduction Convention – A Global View' [2007/08] 41 *Family Law Quarterly* 59.

—— and Ong, D, 'Why the Child Abduction Protocol Negotiations Should Not Deflect Singapore from Acceding to the 1980 Hague Abduction Convention' (2007) *Singapore Journal of Legal Studies* 216.

—— and A Perry, 'International Child Abduction – The English Experience' (1999) 48 *ICLQ* 127.

Macfarlane, D, 'Family Mediation in France' (2004) 10 *Journal of Family Studies* 97.

Masson, J, 'Consent Orders in Contact Cases: A Survey of Resolution Members' (2006) *Family Law* 1042.

McEleavy, P, 'The New Child Abduction Regime in the European Union: Symbiotic Relationship or Forced Partnership?' (2005) 1 *Journal of Private International Law* 5.

—— 'Evaluating the Views of Abducted Children: Trends in Appellate Case Law' (2008) *Child and Family Law Quarterly* 230.

McIntosh, J et al, 'Child-Focused and Child-Inclusive Divorce Mediation: Comparative Outcomes from a Prospective Study of Postseparation Adjustment' (2008) 46 *Family Court Review* 105.

McIntosh, J, Bryant, D and Murray, K, 'Evidence of a Different Nature: The Child-Responsive and Less Adversarial Initiatives of the Family Court of Australia' (2008) 46 *Family Court Review* 125.

Meyer, J and Leathes, M, 'How Mediators Can Obtain Professional Certification and Thereby Elevate Their Profession: A Look at IMI's Voluntary Credentialing Program' (2008) 63(3) *Dispute Resolution Journal.*

Minamikata, S, 'Resolution of Disputes over Parental Rights and Duties in a Marital Dissolution Case in Japan: A Non-Litigious Approach in *Chotei* (Family Court Mediation)' [2005/06] 39 *Family Law Quarterly* 489.

Mnookin, R and Kornhauser, L, 'Bargaining in the Shadow of the Law: The Case of Divorce' (1979) 88 *Yale Law Journal* 950.

O'Brien, S, 'The Trials and Tribulations of Implementing the Hague Convention on International Child Abduction: Improving Dispute Resolution and Enforcement of Parental Rights in the International Arena' (2003) 35 *George Washington International Law Review* 197.

Parkinson, L, 'Child-Inclusive Family Mediation' (2006) *Family Law* 483.

—— 'Mediation Brands: Research from the USA' (2007) *International Family Law* 46.

—— 'Council of Europe 7th European Conference: International Family Mediation' (2009) *International Family Law* 123.

Paul, C and Kaesler, S, 'Mediation within the Framework of a German-English Child Abduction' (2007) 9 *ADR Bulletin* 87.

Paul, C and Walker, J, 'Family Mediation in International Child Custody Conflicts: The Role of the Consulting Attorneys' (2008) 22 *American Journal of Family Law* 42.

Pawlowski, R, 'Alternative Dispute Resolution for Hague Convention Child Custody Disputes' (2007) 45 *Family Court Review* 302.

Permanent Bureau, 'Recent developments at the Hague Conference on Private International Law' (2007) *International Family Law* 101.

Potter, M, 'The Voice of the Child: Children's 'Rights' in Family Proceedings' (2008) *International Family Law* 140.

Pressdee, P, 'Relocation, Relocation, Relocation: Rigorous Scrutiny Revised' (2008) *Family Law* 220.

Raitt, F, 'Hearing Children in Family Law Proceedings: Can Judges Make a Difference?' (2007) *Child and Family Law Quarterly* 204.

Rešetar, B and Emery, R, 'Children's Rights in European Legal Proceedings: Why Are Family Practices So Different From Legal Theories?'(2008) 46 *Family Court Review* 65.

Roberts, M, 'Third Persons in Family Mediation – Towards a Typology of Practice' (2003) *Mediation in Practice.*

—— 'Family Mediation: The Development of the Regulatory Framework in the United Kingdom' (2005) 22 *Conflict Resolution Quarterly* 509.

—— 'Voluntary Participation in Family Mediation' (2006) *Family Law* 57.
—— 'International Family Mediation and Recommendation No R(98)1: A Chronicle of Expansion Foretold' (2008) *International Family Law* 217.
Ruckman, K, 'Undertakings as Convention Practice: The United States Perspective' (2006) 11 *Judges' Newsletter* 45.
Saclier, C, 'The International Social Service and the 1996 Hague Convention' (2005) 10 *Judges' Newsletter* 36.
Sanchez, E and Kibler-Sanchez, S, 'Empowering Children in Mediation: An Intervention Model' (2004) 42 *Family Court Review* 554.
Scherpe, J, 'Legal Recognition of Foreign Formalised Same-Sex Relationships in the UK' (2007) *International Family Law* 196.
Scherrer, R and Louw, D, 'The Origin and Functioning of the Family Advocate System' (2003) 31 *International Journal of the Sociology of Law* 343.
Schoffer, M, 'Bringing Children to the Mediation Table: Defining a Child's Best Interest in Divorce Mediation' (2005) 43 *Family Court Review* 323.
Schuz, R, 'The Hague Child Abduction Convention: Family Law and Private International Law' (1995) 44 *ICLQ* 771.
—— 'The Hague Child Abduction Convention and Children's Rights' (2002) 12 *Transnational Law & Contemporary Problems* 393.
Setright, H, Devereux, E and Hutchinson, A, 'Discretion, Settlement and Child's Objections Re M (Abduction)' (2008) *Family Law* 230.
Shah-Kazemi, S, 'Cross-Cultural Mediation: A Critical View of the Dynamics of Culture in Family Disputes' (2000) 14 *International Journal of Law Policy and the Family* 326.
Shetty, S and Edleson, J, 'Adult Domestic Violence in Cases of International Parental Child Abduction' (2005) 11 *Violence Against Women* 115.
Silberman, L, 'The Hague Child Abduction Convention Turns 20: Gender Politics and Other Issues' (2000) 33 *New York University Journal of International Law & Politics* 221.
—— 'Patching Up the Abduction Convention' (2003) 38 *Texas International Law Journal* 41.
Skjørten, K and Barlindhaug, R, 'The Involvement of Children in Decisions about Shared Residence' (2007) 21 *International Journal of Law Policy and the Family* 373.
Smart, C, 'From Children's Shoes to Children's Voices' (2002) 40 *Family Court Review* 307.
Szaj, C, 'The Fine Art of Listening: Children's Voices in Custody Proceedings' (2002) 4 *Journal of Law and Family Studies* 131.
Thorpe, M, 'Francophone – Anglophone Judicial Conference' (2007) *International Family Law* 110.
—— 'Interdisciplinarity and Internationality in Modern Family Justice Systems' (2007) *International Family Law* 165.
—— 'Urgency in Child Abduction Cases' (2007) *International Family Law* 163.
Von Dadelszen, P, 'The Lawyer for the Child in New Zealand' (2007) *International Family Law* 129.
—— 'Legal Representation of the Child in International Child Abduction Cases' (2009) *International Family Law* 152.
Vonfelt, G, 'International Mediation for Families and the Hague Convention of 25 October 1980' (2006) 11 *Judges' Newsletter* 55.

—— 'How Can Mediation be Developed within the Framework of the Hague Convention of 25 October 1980?' (2007) 12 *Judges' Newsletter* 44.

Walter, M, 'Toward the Recognition and Enforcement of Decisions Concerning Transnational Parent-Child Contact' (2004) 79 *New York University Journal of International Law & Politics* 2381.

Weiner, M, 'International Child Abduction and the Escape from Domestic Violence' (2000) 69 *Fordham Law Review* 593.

—— 'Symposium: The Potential and Challenges of Transnational Litigation for Feminists concerned about Domestic Violence Here and Abroad' (2003) 11 *American University Journal of Gender Society, Policy and the Law* 749.

—— 'Intolerable Situations and Counsel for Children: Following Switzerland's Example in Hague Abduction Cases' (2008) 58 *American University Law Review* 335.

Willis, T, 'Mediator Accreditation: Is it a Risk? Or Quality Enhancement?' (2008) 26 *Alternatives to the High Cost of Litigation* 165.

Wills, M, 'Interpreting the Hague Convention: Why American Courts Need to Reconcile the Rights of Non-Custodial Parents, the Best Interests of Abducted Children, and the Underlying Objectives of the Hague Convention' (2006) 25 *Review of Litigation* 423.

Wise, M, 'New Developments in Mediation in Scotland' (2009) *International Family Law* 42.

Zawid, J, 'Practical and Ethical Implications of Mediating International Child Abduction Cases: A New Frontier for Mediators' (2008) 40 *University of Miami Inter-American Law Review* 1.

Seminar and Conference Papers

4th World Congress on Family Law and Children's Rights (Cape Town, South Africa, March 2005)

Boshier, P, 'Care and Protection of Children: New Zealand and Australian Experience of Cross-Border Co-operation'.

Bryant, D, 'Care and Protection of Children: Australian and New Zealand Experience'.

Carl, E, 'Giving Children Their Own Voice in Family Court Proceedings: A German Perspective'.

Davel, C, 'Exploring the Implication of Article 12 of the United Nations Convention on the Rights of the Child for Legal Practice and Legal Process: The Child's Right to Participate in Legal Proceedings'.

Demson, S and Huddart, J, 'Listening to Children in the Collaborative Process'.

Graham, D, 'The Voice of Children – How Can We Hear It?'.

Henaghan, M, 'Children and Lawyers Acting for Children in Legal Proceedings – What Does a Child's Right to be Heard in Legal Proceedings Really Mean?'.

Henry, A, 'Mediating Child Protection Disputes – A Canadian Perspective: Are We Leaving Room for the Child at the Table?'

J Walker, J, 'Children and Legal Processes'.

ERA Conference on Divorce Mediation (Trier, Germany, March 2005)

Hutchinson, A, 'Can Mediation Play a Role in Cases of International Parental Child Abduction?'.
Todorova, V, 'Possibilities and Limits of Family Mediation: The Case of Bulgaria'.

ERA Conference on Cross-Border Family Mediation (Trier, Germany, April 2007)

Carter, D, 'The Work and Role of reunite and the reunite Mediation Service'.
Niemeijer, B and Pel, M, 'Court-Based Mediation in the Netherlands: Research, Evaluation and Future Expectations'.
Parkinson, L, 'Cross-border Family Mediation: Opportunities, Difficulties and Experience'.
Scholten, M, 'The role of the court and the situation in The Netherlands'.
Thorpe, M, 'The Role of the Judge in International Mediation'.
—— 'The Case for Judicial Activism'.
Tomás García, I, 'Médiation de famille en Espagne'.
Verougstraete, I. 'GEMME'.

7th Council of Europe European Conference on Family Law – 'International Family Mediation' (Strasbourg, France, March 2009)

Alles, S, 'Franco-German Family Mediation: From the Experience of a Parliamentary Pilot Project to New Prospects'.
Arsić, J, 'Family Mediation Concerning Couples of Different Ethnic Origin in the Region of Former Yugoslavia'.
Bustelo, D, 'Family Mediation in Ibero-America'.
Conceiçao Oliveira, M, 'Guidelines for a Better Implementation of the Existing Recommendations Concerning Family Mediation and Mediation in Civil Matters, and Good Practices in Cross-border Family Conflict Mediation'.
Fiadjoe, A, 'Family Mediation in the Caribbean'.
Guiraud Terrier, E, 'Challenges of Training in International Family Mediation in the Light of Experience of the 'Diplôme d'État' in Family Mediation'.
Keshavjee, M, 'Family Mediation in the Shia Imami Ismaili Muslim Community – Institutional Structures, Training and Practice'.
Khazova, O, 'Prospects of International Family Mediation in Russia'.
Kiesewetter, S, 'Emerging Good Practices in the Polish-German Mediation Project'.
Kleim, M, 'The Work of the European Parliament Mediation Office'.
Mouttet, A, 'Une formation européenne de qualité adaptée aux spécificités de la médiation familiale internationale'.
Parkinson, L, 'Developing International Family Mediation and Harmonising Standards'.
Paul, C, 'Mediation in German-United States Cases – A Chance for the Children and Challenge for the Mediators'.

Tell, O, 'La nouvelle Directive 2008/52/CE sur certains aspects de la médiation en matière civile et commerciale outil de promotion de la médiation familiale internationale'.

International Family Justice Judicial Conference for Common Law and Commonwealth Jurisdictions (Windsor, England, August, 2009)

Duncan, W, 'Future Developments in International Family Law, with special emphasis on Cross-border Child Protection – A view from The Hague'.
McGuinness, C, 'The Voice of the Child in Irish Cases on the Hague Convention on Child Abduction 1980'.
Moylan, A, 'The Strengths and Weaknesses of the Hague Convention: A 'Child-Centric' View from an English Judge'.
Schuz, R, 'The Impact of the United Nations Convention on the Rights of the Child on Decision-Making under the Hague Convention on the Civil Aspects of International Child Abduction'.

Other Conference Papers

Parkinson, L, 'Family Mediation in Europe – Divided or United?' European Masters in Mediation (Sion, Switzerland, March 2003).
—— '"Mediation is Good for You!" – Reflections on the ethics of mediation' World Mediation Forum Conference IV (Buenos Aires, Argentina, May 2003).
Singer, P, 'International Child Abduction – Assessing Progress and Planning for the Future' ICMEC Forum (The Hague, The Netherlands, October 2004).

Conclusions of Seminars and Declarations

Conclusions of the Special Commission of May 2000 on General Affairs and Policy of the Conference' Prel. Doc. No 10/2000.
Conclusions and Recommendations of the Fourth Meeting of the Special Commission to Review the Operation of the Hague Convention of 25 October 1980 on the Civil Aspects of International Child Abduction (The Hague, The Netherlands, March 2001).
Conclusions and Recommendations of the International Judicial Seminar on the 1980 Hague Convention on the Civil Aspects of International Child Abduction (De Ruwenberg, The Netherlands, October 2001).
Conclusions and Recommendations of the Judges' Seminar on the 1980 Hague Convention on the Civil Aspects of International Child Abduction (Noordwijk, The Netherlands, October 2003).
Conclusions of the Special Commission of 3–5 April 2006 on General Affairs and Policy of the Conference.

Conclusions and Recommendations of the Fifth Meeting of the Special Commission to Review the Operation of the Hague Convention of 25 October 1980 on the Civil Aspects of International Child Abduction and the Practical Implementation of the Hague Convention of 19 October 1996 on Jurisdiction, Applicable Law, Recognition, Enforcement and Co-operation in respect of Parental Responsibility and Measures for the Protection of Children (The Hague, The Netherlands, October–November 2006).
Conclusions and Recommendations of the Council on General Affairs and Policy of the Conference (The Hague, The Netherlands, April 2008).
Conclusions and Recommendations of the joint Hague Conference and European Community Conference on Direct Judicial Communications on Family Law Matters and the Development of Judicial Network' (Brussels, Belgium, January 2009).
Third Malta Judicial Conference on Cross-Frontier Family Law Issues, hosted by the Government of Malta in collaboration with the Hague Conference on Private International Law (St Julian's, Malta, March 2009).
Wrocław Declaration on Mediation of Bi-national Disputes over Parents' and Children's Issues (Wroclaw, Poland, October 2007).

Reports

Council of Europe

Explanatory Memorandum to Recommendation No R (98) 1 of the Committee of Ministers to Member States on Family Mediation (adopted by the Committee of Ministers on 21 January 1998 at the 616th meeting of the Ministers' Deputies).
Working Group on Mediation 'Analysis on assessment of the impact of Council of Europe recommendations concerning mediation' CEPEJ (2007) (Strasbourg, France, May 2007).

European Community

Practice Guide for the application of the new Brussels II Regulation.

Hague Conference

Collated Responses to the Questionnaire concerning the Practical Operation of the Hague Convention of 25 October 1980 on the Civil Aspects of International Child Abduction, Prel. Doc. No 2/2006.
Comments Received on the Proposal by Switzerland for a Protocol to the Hague Convention of 25 October 1980 on the Civil Aspects of International Child Abduction Prel. Doc. No 12/2008.
Conclusions of the Special Commission of March 1979 on Legal Kidnapping in *Actes et documents de la quatorzième session, Tome III, Enlèvement d'enfants* (The Hague, Hague Conference, 1982).

Duncan, W, 'Transfrontier Access/Contact – General Principles and Good Practice' Prel. Doc. No 4/2006.

Dyer, A, 'Report on International Child Abduction by one Parent ('Legal Kidnapping')' Prel. Doc. No 1/1978 in *Actes et documents de la quatorzième session, Tome III, Enlèvement d'enfants* (The Hague, Hague Conference, 1982).

Gosselain, C, 'Child Abduction and Transfrontier Access: Bilateral Conventions and Islamic States – A Research Paper' Prel. Doc. No 7/2002.

Feasibility Study on Cross-Border Mediation in Family Matters Prel. Doc. No 20/2007.

Feasibility Study on Cross Border Mediation in Family Matters – Responses to the Questionnaire Prel. Doc. No 10/2008.

Hague Conference on Private International Law, *Actes et documents de la treizième session, Tome I, Matières diverses* (The Hague, Hague Conference, 1978).

Hague Conference on Private International Law 'Guide to Good Practice under the Hague Convention of 25 October 1980 on the Civil Aspects of International Child Abduction – Part I – Central Authority Practice' (Bristol, Family Law, 2003).

Hague Conference on Private International Law, 'Guide to Good Practice under the Hague Convention of 25 October 1980 on the Civil Aspects of International Child Abduction – Part II – Implementing Measures' (Bristol, Family Law, 2003).

Hague Conference on Private International Law, 'Guide to Good Practice under the Hague Convention of 25 October 1980 on the Civil Aspects of International Child Abduction – Part III – Preventive Measures' (Bristol, Family Law, 2005).

Hague Conference on Private International Law, 'General Principles and Guide to Good Practice on Transfrontier Contact Concerning Children' (Bristol, Family Law, 2008).

International Social Service, 'Summary of Findings on a Questionnaire Studied by International Social Service' Prel. Doc. No 3/1979 in *Actes et documents de la quatorzième session, Tome III, Enlèvement d'enfants* (The Hague, Hague Conference, 1982).

Lagard, P, 'Explanatory Report to the Hague Convention of 19 October 1996 on Jurisdiction, Applicable Law, Recognition, Enforcement and Co-operation in respect of Parental Responsibility and Measures for the Protection of Children' in *Actes et documents de la dix-huitième session, Tome II, Protection des enfants* (The Hague, Hague Conference, 1996).

Lortie, P, 'Report on Judicial Communications in relation to International Child Protection' Prel. Doc. No 8/2006.

Lowe, N et al, 'A Statistical Analysis of Applications made in 2003 under the Hague Convention of 25 October 1980 on the Civil Aspects of International Child Abduction: Part I: Overall Report (2007 update)' Prel. Doc. No 3/2006.

—— 'A Statistical Analysis of Applications made in 2003 under the Hague Convention of 25 October 1980 on the Civil Aspects of International Child Abduction: Part II: National Reports (2007 update)' Prel. Doc. No 3/2006.

Lowe, N, Armstrong, S and Mathias, A, 'A Statistical Analysis of Applications made in 1999 under the Hague Convention of 25 October 1980 on the Civil Aspects of International Child Abduction (revised version, November 2001)' Prel. Doc. No 3/2001.

Pérez-Vera, E, 'Explanatory Report to the Hague Convention of 25 October 1980 on the Civil Aspects of International Child Abduction' in *Actes et documents de la quatorzième session, Tome III, Enlèvement d'enfants* (The Hague, Hague Conference, 1982).

Questionnaire concerning the Practical Operation of the Hague Convention of 25 October 1980 on the Civil Aspects of International Child Abduction (including questions on implementation of the Hague Convention of 19 October 1996 on Jurisdiction, Applicable

Law, Recognition, Enforcement and Co-operation in respect of Parental Responsibility and Measures for the Protection of Children), Prel. Doc. No 1/2006.
Report on the Fifth Meeting of the Special Commission to Review the Operation of the Hague Convention of 25 October 1980 on the Civil Aspects of International Child Abduction and the Practical Implementation of the Hague Convention of 19 October 1996 on Jurisdiction, Applicable Law, Recognition, Enforcement and Co-operation in Respect of Parental Responsibility and Measures for the Protection of Children (The Hague, The Netherlands, October–November 2006) Prel. Doc. No 19/2007.
Schulz, A, 'Enforcement of Orders made under the 1980 Convention – A Comparative Legal Study' Prel. Doc. No 6/2006.
—— 'Enforcement of Orders made under the 1980 Convention – Towards Principles of Good Practice' Prel. Doc. No 7/2006.
Vigers, S, 'Note on the Development of Mediation, Conciliation and Similar Means to Facilitate Agreed Solutions in Transfrontier Family Disputes Concerning Children Especially in the Context of the Hague Convention of 1980' Prel. Doc. No 5/2006.

International Social Service

Auerbach, S, 'The Mediation Based Approach' (ISS Switzerland, Annual Report, 2005).
International Social Service, Australian Branch 'Living in Limbo – The experience of international parental child abduction – the call for a national support service' (February 2005).
International Social Service Switzerland, International Social Service Germany & International Social Service General Secretariat 'Children in Cross-border Family Conflicts the Approach of International Social Service for Facilitating Amicable Solutions in their Best Interests in the Context of the Hague Conventions of 1980 and 1996' (Geneva/Berlin, August 2006).

The Joseph Rowntree Foundation

Dunn, J and Deater-Deckard, K, 'Children's views of their changing families' (2001).
Hawthorne, J et al, 'Supporting children through family change: A review of interventions and services for children of divorcing and separating parents' (2003).
Henricson, C and Bainham, A, 'The Child and Family Policy Divide: Tensions, Convergence and Rights' (2005).
McCarthy, P and Walker, J, 'The Longer Term Impact of Family Mediation' (2006).
O'Quigley, A, 'Listening to Children's Views: The Findings and Recommendations of Recent Research' (2000).
Trinder, L, Beek, M and Connolly, J, 'Making contact: How parents and children negotiate and experience contact after divorce' (2002).
Wade, A and Smart, C, 'Facing Family Change: Children's Circumstances, Strategies and Resources' (2002).

Reunite

Freeman, M (for the reunite Research Unit), 'International Child Abduction – The Effects' (May 2006).

reunite Research Unit, 'The Outcomes for Children Returned Following an Abduction' (September 2003).

reunite, 'Mediation in International Parental Child Abduction – The reunite Mediation Pilot Scheme' (October 2006).

Other reports

Civil and Family Law Policy Office, 'Family Relations Act Review, Children's Participation' (April 2007) (Canada).

Craig, J, '"Everybody's Business" – How applications for contact orders by consent should be approached by the court in cases involving domestic violence' The Family Justice Council's Report and Recommendations to the President of the Family Division (February 2007).

Department of State, Office of Children's Issues, 'Report on Compliance with the Hague Convention on the Civil Aspects of International Child Abduction' (April 2007) (United States).

Department of State, Office of Children's Issues, 'Report on Compliance with the Hague Convention on the Civil Aspects of International Child Abduction' (April 2008) (United States).

Goldson, J, 'Hello I'm a Voice Let Me Talk: Child-Inclusive Mediation in Family Separation' Innovative Practice Report No 1/06 (December 2006).

Legal Services Commission, 'Publicly Funded Family Mediation: the Way Forward: The Legal Services Commission's Strategy for Family Mediation' (August 2008) (England and Wales).

Lowe, N and Horosova, K, 'Good Practice Report on Access Under the Hague Convention of 25 October 1980 on the Civil Aspects of International Child Abduction' (2007).

McIntosh, J and Long, C, 'Children beyond dispute: A prospective study of outcomes from child focused and child inclusive post-separation family dispute resolution' (Final Report) (October 2006).

McIntosh, J and Long, C, 'The Child Responsive Program Pilot, within the Less Adversarial Trial: A follow up study of parent and child outcomes' (July 2007) (Australia).

National Audit Office, 'Legal Services Commission: Legal Aid and Mediation for People Involved in Family Breakdown' HC 256 Session 2006-07 (March 2007) (England and Wales).

Stimec, A,'La co-médiation familale internationale en navette' Service social d'aide aux emigrants' (May 2002).

Van Bueren, G, '*The Best Interests of the Child – International Co-operation on Child Abduction*' (The British Institute of Human Rights, Programme of the International Rights of the Child, Reunite: National Council for Abduction Children) Programme on the International Rights of the Child (1993).

Primary and Secondary Legislation

International and Regional Instruments

Council Regulation (EC) 2201/2003 of 27 November 2003 concerning jurisdiction and the recognition and enforcement of judgments in matrimonial matters and the matters of parental responsibility, repealing Regulation (EC) No 1347/2000 [2003] OJ338/2.

Directive 2008/52/EC of the European Parliament and of the Council of 21 May 2008 on certain aspects of mediation in civil and commercial matters.

European Code of Conduct for Mediators (Brussels, Belgium July 2004) http://ec.europa.eu/civiljustice/adr/adr_ec_code_conduct_en.htm.

European Convention on Contact Concerning Children (adopted 15 May 2003, entered into force 1 September 2005) ETS No 192.

European Convention on the Exercise of Children's Rights (adopted 25 January 1996, entered into force 1 July 2000) ETS No 160.

European Convention for the Protection of Human Rights and Fundamental Freedoms (adopted 4 November 1950, entered into force 3 September 1953) ETS No 5.

European Convention on Recognition and Enforcement of Decisions concerning Custody of Children and on Restoration of Custody of Children of 20 May 1980 (adopted 20 May 1980, entered into force 1 September 1983) ETS No 105.

Hague Convention Abolishing the Requirement of Legalisation for Foreign Public Documents (adopted 5 October 1961, entered into force 24 January 1965) 527 UNTS 189.

Hague Convention on the Civil Aspects of International Child Abduction (adopted 25 October 1980, entered into force 1 December 1983) 1343 UNTS 89.

Hague Convention on the International Recovery of Child Support and Other Forms of Family Maintenance (concluded 23 November 2007).

Hague Convention on Jurisdiction, Applicable Law, Recognition, Enforcement and Co-operation in respect of Parental Responsibility and Measures for the Protection of Children (adopted 19 October 1996, entered into force 1 January 2002) 35 ILM 1391.

Recommendation No R(98)1 of the Committee of Ministers to Member States on Family Mediation (adopted by the Committee of Ministers on 21 January 1998) (Council of Europe).

Recommendation Rec (2002)10 of the Committee of Ministers to Member States on Mediation in Civil Matters (Adopted by the Committee of Ministers on 18 September 2002) (Council of Europe).

United Nations Convention on the Rights of the Child (adopted 20 November 1989, entered into force 2 September 1990) 1577 UNTS 3.

Domestic Legislation and Regulation

Act on Recognition and Enforcement of Foreign Decisions concerning Custody, etc., and on the Return of Children (1989:14) (Sweden).

Arrêté fédéral portant mise en œuvre des conventions sur l'enlèvement international d'enfants et portant approbation et mise en œuvre des Conventions de La Haye sur la protection des enfants et des adultes du 21 décembre 2007, Feuille Fédérale no. 1 (2008) 33-40 RS 211.222.32 (Switzerland).

Children Act 1989 (England and Wales).

Civil Evidence (Family Mediation) (Scotland) Act 1995.

Model Standards of Conduct for Mediators 2005, adopted by the American Arbitration Association (8 September 2005), American Bar Association (9 August 2005), and the Association for Conflict Resolution (22 August 2005) (United States).

Model Standards of Practice for Family and Divorce Mediation, developed by the Association of Family and Conciliatory Courts, the Family Law Section of the American Bar Association, and the national Council of Dispute Resolution Organizations (August 2000) (United States).

Uniform Mediation Act drafted by the National Conference of Commissioners on Uniform State Laws 2001(last revised or amended in 2003) (United States).

INDEX

www.ingramcontent.com/pod-product-compliance
Lightning Source LLC
Chambersburg PA
CBHW071246180926
51613CB00007B/267/J
9781849461818